Queen of the Sheep

(NEW WRITING SCOTLAND 23)

Edited by
Valerie Thornton
and
Hamish Whyte
with Maoilios Caimbeul (Gaelic Adviser)

Association for Scottish Literary Studies

Association for Scottish Literary Studies
c/o Department of Scottish History, 9 University Gardens
University of Glasgow, Glasgow G12 8QH
www.asls.org.uk

First published 2005

© Association for Scottish Literary Studies
and the individual contributors

British Library Cataloguing in Publication Data

A CIP record for this book is available
from the British Library

ISBN 0–948877–69–3

The Association for Scottish Literary Studies
acknowledges the support of the Scottish Arts Council
towards the publication of this book

Typeset by AFS Image Setters Ltd, Glasgow

Printed by Bell & Bain Ltd, Glasgow

CONTENTS

Tom Bryan	Hey, Eddie Rae	7
Jim Carruth	Queen of the Sheep	8
	The Moleman's Apprentice	9
	Island Rhythms	10
	264	11
Ken Cockburn	On the Flyleaf of *Yves Klein*	12
	On the Flyleaf of *Submariner #36*	14
Neil Cocker	Landfill	16
Michael Coutts	Douggie's Thoughts	23
James Cressey	Urchin	27
Alexander Cuthbert	The Impossibility of Pure Water	30
Vicki Feaver	Sloes	33
	Green	34
Graham Fulton	Remainders	35
	This Is Your Life	36
Rab Swannock Fulton	ahm grinnin lik an eejit	38
Robin Fulton	Octet	39
	The River Helmsdale	39
	Geography Lessons	40
Iain Galbraith	Blue Wings	41
Mark Gallacher	The Miles	42
Paul Gorman	A Swarming	51
Rody Gorman	Frank O'Hara: Dàn	54
	Cuileag-shneachda	54
	Dìreach gus a Ràdh	55
	Gluasad	56
	Shingle	56
Charlie Gracie	Rain	57
Rosemary Hector	Brent Millar's Lovebirds	58
Kate Hendry	All That Glass	59
Sonja Henrici	Waiting for Neptune	65
John Heraghty	Falling	66
Duncan Jones	Urban Myths	72
Beth Junor	Asunder	77
	Winter Solstice	78
Kirsten Kearney	Psalm 23	79
Lis Lee	Bush Fire	80

Joanna Lilley	thief	81
	disappointment	81
	emigrant	82
Stuart Robert MacDonald	Jock Steinbeck on Rue Osgoode, Ottawa	83
	Aceto Balsamico di Modena	85
Morag McDowell	Pondlife	86
James McGonigal	The Camphill Wren	94
	Preparations for Easter	95
	The Half-Awake Soul	96
Mora Maclean	Playing Scarecrow	97
	In the Fitting Room	99
Tony McLean	F.FWD	100
Niall MacRath	Dh'Èirich Snathag	107
	Tobhta Ruairidh a' Ghlinne	109
Lyn Moir	Not an Eider Duck	110
Michael Munro	Time for New Stories	111
Donald S. Murray	Hats	112
Siùsaidh NicRath	A' Choinneamh	113
	Ainmhidh	116
Chris Powici	Ewe-Skull	119
Sarah Reynolds	The Visitors	120
R.J. Ritchie	New Words	122
Lydia Robb	Auntie Bean Undresses	123
	Antisyzygy	124
Kirsteen Scott	At the Dance	125
Robert Swift	The Plaited Dog Turd with the Oak-Leaf Sail	126
Judith Taylor	After Sappho	129
	Chicken Poem	130
Sheila Templeton	Calyx for Georgia O'Keeffe	131
	Roasting Vegetables for Lunch	132
Tim Turnbull	The Stockman's Calendar	133
Fiona R. Walker	Inside the Kist	135
	Glacier	136
	Imagining 90	137
Fiona Wilson	First Line	138
Kirsti Wishart	L'Oiseau Mechanique	139
Olga Wojtas	The Ballad of the Starbucks Café	148

INTRODUCTION

Forty-eight contributors this year, slightly down on Issue 21, but with about the same number of pieces. Twenty-seven men, twenty-one women: the gender balance is improving. And a good mixture of well-known, up-and-coming and new names. As ever, it's all new writing and the usual wide range of topics and styles that never fails to amaze.

We have country and city (source of much humour, gallus and gallows); weather (rain, of course) and seasons; Frank O'Hara in Gaelic and Jock Steinbeck in Canada; a few birds (eider, chicken, wren and Brent Millar's lovebirds); food (regularly on the *NWS* menu); sheep (not least Jim Carruth's title poem, the latest in his ongoing series of agriverse) and much more.

Both of us have been involved with *New Writing Scotland* since it began and are sorry to be standing down as editors (Hamish this year, Val next year), but we will continue to submit poems and stories as potential contributors (anonymously, of course!). As editors we have thoroughly enjoyed the process – the discovery of exciting new talent is particularly rewarding. Someone once wrote that an editor is 'nothing more than a highly sensitised reader, the first link in what may be a chain of proliferating impacts.' We're not sure how highly sensitised we are, but we're happy to be that first link.

The previous issue, Number 22, was a compendium of the first twenty issues (and well-received, we may say) and marked a watershed. Number 23 is the start of the next generation of *New Writing Scotland* and we hope it will keep going, reinvigorated – by its publishers, by its editors, by wonderful new work by writers old and new and by you, its readers, the most important link in the chain.

May *New Writing Scotland* live long and prosper!

Valerie Thornton
Hamish Whyte

NEW WRITING SCOTLAND 24

The twenty-fourth volume of *New Writing Scotland* will be published in summer 2006. Submissions are invited from writers resident in Scotland or Scots by birth or upbringing. Poetry, drama, short fiction or other creative prose may be submitted but not full-length plays or novels, though self-contained extracts are acceptable. The work must be neither previously published nor accepted for publication and may be in any of the languages of Scotland.

Submissions should be typed, double-spaced, on one side of the paper only and the sheets secured at the top-left corner. Prose pieces should carry an approximate word-count. **You should provide a covering letter, clearly marked with your name and address. Please do not put your name or other details on the individual works.** If you would like to receive an acknowledgement of receipt of your manuscript, please enclose a stamped addressed postcard. If you would like to be informed if your submission is unsuccessful, or if you would like your submissions returned, you should enclose a stamped addressed envelope with sufficient postage. Submissions should be sent by **30 September 2005**, in an A4 envelope, to the address below. We are sorry but we cannot accept submissions by fax or e-mail.

Please be aware that we have limited space in each edition, and therefore shorter pieces are more suitable – although longer items of exceptional quality may still be included. A maximum length of 3,500 words is suggested. Please send no more than two short stories and no more than six poems.

ASLS
c/o Department of Scottish History
9 University Gardens
University of Glasgow
Glasgow G12 8QH, Scotland

Tel +44 (0)141 330 5309
www.asls.org.uk

Tom Bryan

HEY, EDDIE RAE

Ran like whitewater
down lanes and past
    to here again
and there
down alleys, mud, snow, rain.
Gone to back and nowhere else,
somewhere soon (and fast)

Oh when Eddie Rae was shot
for money he never had,
plenty blood, but officer,
no noise, no screaming?

If I remember Eddie
(pre-bullet)
he was not so fast,
as dreaming.

Jim Carruth

QUEEN OF THE SHEEP

The Queen of the Sheep lies in state
on a small hummock,
in the open air,
through the hottest day of the year.

No long illness,
no special message,
no official announcement,
she just rolled over and died
like many of her kind before:
a pure bred Texel.
Blood lines don't matter
when you're gone.

Laid out in buzzing robes,
inane grin of rotten teeth,
thick rubber tongue.
Black feathered courtiers
bow to her eye sockets.
Her own incense is a rank royal odour.
Death in this heat rules the senses.

Trailing a cortege of flies and crows,
I drag the bloated corpse to the gate
by her small insubstantial legs:
a less than dignified exit.
My cheeks are tracked by sweat not tears.

The followers refuse to rise in the heat
sit around uninterested;
there's always another.
The Queen of the Sheep is dead.
Long live the Queen.

THE MOLEMAN'S APPRENTICE

surfaced one Friday night
at the village hall
and asked her to dance,
leading the way
through the crowded floor,
parting couples
who closed in tight
behind them.
All evening she stared
into his small eyes
felt his first beard
soft furred
against her face,
but now that's not
what she remembers
nor his dirty long nails,
his spade-like hands,
his proud boasting
that in a first week
measured in pelts
he had plucked the dead
from their dark;
instead it's the incident
near the end,
when some joker
flicked a switch
cut the power,
his shudder and scream
as the night snapped shut.

ISLAND RHYTHMS

Exoduuusss
Movement of Jah people
Is what he sings unaccompanied
In the karaoke at Stornoway
For though he asks for Jimmy Cliff,
Toots and the Maytals,
All they ever have is
Blanket on the Ground;
And his Reggae Ceilidh band
Bob Mackintosh and the Whalers:
With their self-proclaimed mission
To bring rhythm and bass
Back into the heart of the psalms
Lasted only one gig
Old Miss Munroe from the post office
Less than pleased to be asked
To take her partner for some lovers' rock
Constable Macleod shocked too
By Bob's confession that he'd shot a sheriff.
However his crocheted reggae hats
Have been an unexpected hit
As working bunnets for crofters across the island
Each its own tiny rainbow
Between overcast skies and bog;
And on Sunday afternoons when it's dry
A small band of loyal followers
Gather to hear him and smoke peat spliffs.
He tells them they're all Africans
Promises the return of Haile Selassie
But does not give a ferry time.
With his hair splayed out in the wind
More matted cow tail than dreadlock
He skanks around the standing stones
Chanting to himself an incantation
I an' I – Wee Free Rastafari,
I an' I – Wee Free Rastafari.

264

During his birthday meal
he gives it to us as a gift;
just announces it
in the middle of a conversation
hangs it there in mid air
above the candles
and plastic tractor on his cake
without the anchor of context:
a riddle for us to solve.
Just one number nothing else
not random either,
he's taken time to work it out
something important to him.
So we start the guessing game:
total days it rained last year;
minutes of sleep he takes each night;
hours between bank manager's calls;
milking cows left in the district.
To each answer he shakes his head.
After ten minutes of attempts
my family lose interest
leave the table.
I keep trying –
Something to do with
acres or tonnage
cattle prices
milk yield.
Frustrated I offer up;
cabbages in the garden;
molehills in the bottom field;
I know they're wrong.
He doesn't even answer
retires to a soft chair
sipping slowly on a small whisky
while grandchildren play at his feet
asks me if I give up.
After a while I do.
He states simply
seasons in my life.

Ken Cockburn

ON THE FLYLEAF OF
YVES KLEIN BY SIDRA STICH
(London: Hayward Gallery, 1994)

Stac Pollaidh: 11 September, 2002

Once you leave the A-road
the pelting rain starts to ease.
Patches of, at first,
the palest blue
spread and intensify.
Still, you assume it won't last,
pull on the serious waterproofs which,
barely into the ascent
and far too hot, you discard.
You climb until shades of meaning
(grasses and the vivid purples
of late summer flowers) pass
and there is only the fissured,
slowly collapsing rock. This
is as high as you're going to get,
though cliffs rise above you; here
you're still mobile and need
no specialist equipment.
You look on moor, loch, sea,
a single-track road snaking west
and your eye picks out a car
making for the coast
which might, it's hard to tell,
be blue; and a shrine, though maybe
you just imagine this,
dedicated to
St Rita, patron saint
of the impossible,
set against the tumbling
pebbles of the long Atlantic.
Vo–lare, oh–oh,
Cantare, oh-oh-oh-oh...

Reception, despite the mountains,
is clear, and if the vehicle
shimmers through the birches'
uncertainty, the sky
is unambiguous.

ON THE FLYLEAF OF *SUBMARINER, #36* (Marvel Comics, 1971)

Once at Easter or maybe autumn
with the railway-line on my right
and on my left the flat silver-grey of the firth
I walked past Stark's Park and the Teil Burn
across the Auchtertool road
almost as far as the colliery gates
(the road running on till it twisted
under the railway-bridge and uphill)
to the paper-shop which I'd found stocked everything

Captain Marvel, Iron Man, Doctor Doom,
the Daredevil, the Avengers and the X-Men,
occasional villains who'd been transformed
into titular if flawed heroes, mutants
whose power derived as likely as not
from an accident in the lab
(a touch of the Jekylls about most of them)
and which, whatever it enabled them to achieve,
removed them from the everyday ground

and there were those of mythical stock
like Atlantean Namor the Submariner
whose real source of power whatever
superhuman strength he had accrued
lay in his uncontrollable rage
and though I don't remember much of the story
I remember that when he found at the end of #36
his wife fatally injured and at the start of #37
his wife untransformably dead, I understood
whether or not she'd appear in the odd flashback
neither willpower nor weird science would resurrect her.

Now, passing through on the train
no shop to be seen and the pit
long since closed, I imagine
the abandoned tunnels that run for miles
beneath the sea-bed, and think
how deceptively easy it was in the end to leave,
and that however you try to return (willpower
or weird science), the scene's as altered as was, say,
the original Doctor Strange from his later, redrawn, self.

Neil Cocker

LANDFILL

'Aw shite!'

He'd forgotten to apply the Vaseline. McFall gritted his teeth. This was going to be painful.

Wednesday's run had been bad. Eight miles of agony, t-shirt fabric happily sand-papering the tips off his nipples, a trickle of blood from the left one like his heart was weeping. He had vowed then that something had to be done.

He'd planned it meticulously, driving all the way out to the retail park and into the anonymity of Sainsbury's. It was not an option to buy Vaseline in his local Co-op. It was a year since the divorce and he didn't want to start a whispering campaign in the town.

His feet slapped through the puddles as he ran, his Reeboks splashing from muddy water to gravel, muddy water to gravel. McFall cursed himself again. The track got steeper, and he lowered his head, ready for pain. The hill was up ahead, ten minutes of slog, and then after that the gentle downhill stretch past the stench of the landfill.

So he'd gone into Sainsbury's and taken a wee green basket and wandered up the aisles filling it with the trappings of the single man: crisps, microwave lasagne, chocolate mousses, vitamin tablets. And when he had enough camouflage in the basket he'd wandered over to the pharmacy section, taken a jar of Vaseline casually off the shelf, and hid it under his Salt n' Vinegar multipack.

At the check-out he'd watched as the assistant bleeped his shopping through. The Vaseline went unnoticed and he wedged it down into the poly bag out of sight. Then the check-out girl spoke to him.

'That's twelve,' she said.

'Eh?'

She pointed to the sign overhead: TEN ITEMS OR LESS. He frowned, thinking. And then just like he told Fiona, he said it wouldn't happen again.

Sweat was running into his eyes. McFall ducked his head

against his shoulder and blotted his forehead against his t-shirt. His calf muscles were straining, jarring against the impact. He looked over to the hillside at the sheep and scree, the cairn that marked the halfway stage. Any minute now the bitter-foul smell from the landfill would waft over, putrid and cabbagey, and unable to stop himself he would gulp in the stinking air and feel it lie heavy in his lungs.

The friction had started. Left, right, left, right, left... as his feet pounded the track his t-shirt plucked at his scabbed nipples, and he tried to think about something else, his usual tactic when encountering discomfort. Sainsbury's... what was the check-out girl's name? But instead of Sainsbury's his mind jumped to Fiona, and the day she told him it was all over.

Him bouncing off the walls as he went up the tenement stairs, chilli sauce on his chin and whisky on his breath. Fumbling his key into the lock and letting his jacket slide off his shoulders onto the hall floor. And into the kitchen where she sat with her parents and wee Amy, them all looking at photograph albums and him swaying in an imaginary wind. The look in her eyes that suddenly said no more. No more dried vomit down the side of the toilet, no more mystery condoms in his wallet, no more forgetting the wee one's birthday. We won three-nil, he had said.

The top of the hill was in sight. McFall bit his lip, hoping the image of her would fade. He was cursed with a photographic memory. It was like the angelic side of his brain had made a photograph album of all of his mistakes, and took it upon itself to run through them every once in a while.

Nearly at the top, the scab coming away from the nipple, wet pain seeping.

After the separation and moving to the bedsit, weeks of lost nights and headache mornings. Working for a whisky company didn't help. He was lucky he'd never got caught, fiddling the paperwork and sneaking cases from the storeroom out to the car park when it got dark. He only stole *Laddie of the Loch*, a dodgy blend the company sold exclusively in Thailand. Bangkok brothel mouthwash, his workmates said. For him it had been mindwash. Rinse away the memories and spit them out.

He'd stopped stealing whisky when being drunk got boring. Standing around in pubs with his fat single friends, talking about football and cars and porn. Increasingly haunted by the nice things Fiona used to do for him: cut his hair, iron his shirts, leave a sandwich in the fridge for him when she went to aerobics. And then worse images visited him: wee Amy without a dad. Fifteen minutes he'd spent crying in the toilet at work when he first thought of that one.

So one night, he started running. Huffing through the streets of the town, beergut swinging like a sack of potatoes. Car horns honking and yells in the street. Head down, blinded by sweat, he kept going. The beergut deflated after a month. He liked running: the blisters, the ripped lungs, the stitches. He liked having a pain he was in control of.

The track broadened as it reached the peak. He felt elated: from here it was a gentle slope back down past the landfill and then through the wood and over the river. He felt weird too, suddenly realising he now had quite a lot in common with Fiona: he was off drink, and he didn't like his friends. And hadn't she complained about sore nipples?

He grinned as he rounded the bend, but the smile froze on his face when he heard the gunshot.

A dry thump and then a jolting echo, gouging a silence from the empty hillsides. He frowned. He had been running this route for two months and had never seen any sign of life, except for a distant bulldozer ploughing through the sea of binbags.

As he continued on the track, stride faltering, he heard another gunshot. Closer, the echo bouncing in a different direction. Down below to his left the gulls scattered from the landfill, shreds of white puffing up like feathers from a burst cushion. What was there to shoot up here? Rabbits? Maybe deer?

The track tilted downwards and he felt himself speed up. This was the last section of the track to hug the hillside. He would soon come onto the plateau that dropped away to the ocean of rubbish.

He rounded the bend and skidded to a halt, pitching forward onto his toes.

LANDFILL

A four wheel drive blocked the track, mud smeared over the radiator. In front stood two men: one small and wearing a suit and overcoat, one bulky and holding a snapped-open shotgun. And in front of them, at their feet, two dead men, hands bound behind their backs, split heads bleeding dark into a puddle.

'Fuck,' said the bulky man.

'Shoot him,' said the little man.

McFall's legs took over. He ran down to the left and vaulted the dry-stane dike, feet landing on the rough ground, tumbling him forward, bundling him down the scree. Angry voices from overhead. The air tore open with a gunshot and metal rained through the gorse as he kept on tumbling, down through ripping thorns and jagged rocks, world spinning dizzily. He banged to a halt on grass rutted with wheel tracks, the air slapped from his lungs. The sky trembled overhead and another gunshot flew past, skittering against a rock.

To his left were mounds of displaced earth, and beyond that nothing; to his right, open ground. Below him were the slagheaps and canyons of rubbish. He jumped over the edge.

Two seconds of nothingness, just a rush of air and empty silence. Then *oooomph*, the smack of binbag plastic, like hitting a beanbag with a broken umbrella inside it. He groaned and rolled off the top of the pile and surfed headfirst down the slope, the plastic snatching at his bare legs, and flopped to a halt next to a burst binbag. Gulls fluttered and scrawked away from their pickings. McFall looked at the guts of the disembowelled black sack: tampons, a banana skin, biscuit wrappers, beer cans. Wheezing, breath returning, lungs filling with the stink. From above, the wind carried down the angry voices.

He tried to sit up, but it was difficult. His t-shirt was torn and bloody, and his whole body was covered with scratches and grazes. He hobbled to his feet. The voices got closer. He looked back up to where he had jumped from but all he could see was the towering pile of black bags.

The voices were close enough to hear.

'The fucker jumped doon there.'

'Well, go doon an fuckin get him!'

'Fuck off! Look at the mess.'

'D'ye want tae go tae prison when that wee jogger cunt tells the polis aboot us? Eh?'
'Right, but ye're comin wi me.'
McFall spotted the carpet. It was frayed and stained, with a faded sunflower design. It had obviously been rolled up when it arrived at the landfill but had since unravelled across the foot of the mountain of rubbish. He limped over and peeled back the edge: underneath was some older rubbish, brown and withered. He crawled into the hollow and let the carpet drop over him.
Darkness. Stinking darkness. And then the flumping noise of someone landing on the bin bags up above.
'Fuck!'
Another flumping noise. Another curse.
McFall closed his eyes. The stench was unbelievable. Rotten veg, foosty milk, dogshit, cat piss, sour puke. His face was an inch away from the carpet. It stank as well, decades of cigarette smoke mingling with the other smells. He gagged, his stomach tightening, and put a hand over his mouth and nose.
Footsteps slogged somewhere above, dislodging scatters of rubbish down onto his carpet roof. And the voices again.
'This is your fault.'
'How is it my fuckin fault?'
'Why don't ye use a proper gun? An automatic, instead o fannyin around wi that shotgun like ye're in The Untouchables.'
'Fuck off.'
'Don't tell me tae fuck off ya fat bastard.'
McFall clenched his hand into the rubbish, trying to hold his breath. It was like listening to his friends. Like being back in that Wotherspoon's pub they liked to go to, like listening to one of their tired and unfunny arguments.
His nails dug into something soft. He probed with his fingertips at the shape, feeling the soft contours. Padded. Crumpled. Crusty. It felt like a dried out nappy.
And he started thinking about wee Amy.

A time in Sainsbury's, cruising up and down the aisles with Fiona, him pushing an overburdened trolley stacked high with Pampers and jars and tins, wee Amy sitting in her special chair propped on the trolley, watching him with big brown eyes. Fiona was over looking at cereal packets. And he leaned over to Amy and kissed her on the eyebrow. Who would have thought a wee baby would need so much stuff? She looked back up at him, snot shining on her upper lip, awe in her eyes.

'Let's just go back, eh. It's worse that somebody sees the bodies up there. They call the polis an we're fucked. The jogger never had time tae see the registration anyway.'
  'Shut up. He's no far away. We're gonnae find him. ARE YE LISTENIN YA CUNT! WE'RE COMIN TAE FUCKIN SHOOT YE!'

McFall remembered lots of times in the supermarket. He used to quite like going. He knew the switch card would take a battering but it was alright. There was a comfort in seeing the car boot full of crinkled white poly bags. And on the drive home, Amy giggling and squealing in the back, while him and Fiona argued in the front.
  He'd last seen them waiting at the traffic lights next to the town cross. Fiona looked good, wearing a lot of her old studenty gear, the duffel coat he'd always liked and cargo pants and clubby trainers. He sat in the car watching them. Amy clapping her hands over her tiny head and Fiona staring ahead pretending she couldn't see the car. The lights changed to green and still he sat there. He'd felt like his body was an empty shell, inside the empty shell of the car, inside the empty shell of the world. Like Russian dolls. An Eddie Stobart truck beeped behind him and he eased off, catching the last sight of them sliding by in the wing mirror.

'Have ye loaded the gun?'
  'Aye.'
  'Is there many cartridges left?'
  'One or two.'
  'One or two!'
  'Look, ye never telt me ah would have tae shoot a fuckin jogger as well.'
  McFall trembled uncontrollably. The stink had gone up his nostrils and was in his throat. His stomach churned, and he was beginning to panic, eyes open but only seeing blind

darkness, the twine of the carpet rubbing against his forehead.

'Where is the bastard?'

'He's hidin, eh. There's naewhere tae go doon here. He's no far away.'

If they hadn't been on the track he would be nearly home by now. He would have jogged past the burn, gushing with the spring rainfall, and through the bluebell wood. He would have run past the war memorial and up McEwan Street. He would be back in the bedsit, the blood pounding in his head, sweat-slick on his body, adrenalin buzz tingling. And then a lukewarm shower, throwing on his baggiest clothes, and standing in the quiet of the untended garden, listening to the birds and the distant swish of passing cars.

'Just fuckin stand still for a wee bit and listen. He cannae be far.'

In the darkness of his garbage underworld, McFall froze. Something was wriggling against his leg. Rough fur, whiskers maybe, scribbling on his skin, a warmth scurrying into his thigh.

'Will ye stop yer heavy breathin, ya fat bastard! Ahm tryin tae listen!'

McFall moaned and kicked his leg away from the creature. His foot hit the carpet and it lurched up, allowing a brief glimpse of light before it flopped back down again.

The gun roared.

A heaviness crushed down on McFall, a smothering blackness.

Dead, he thought.

Then, a lone voice. 'That's the last time ye call me a fat bastard.'

And footsteps began to climb away from McFall, heavy movements through rustling rubbish. He lay still and listened to his heartbeat, imagining that the steady thud was his feet slapping the ground, his Reeboks dancing through the puddles. The weight of the body pressed down on his chest, and he shifted his head forward so that he could breathe properly. Tears ran down his face and into his mouth, saltwater on his tongue. Somewhere up above an engine started, and he listened as it droned away into nothingness, until the only noise was the keening of the gulls.

Michael Coutts

DOUGGIE'S THOUGHTS

When I ask Dad what the computer does, he says: 'It thinks fast, faster than you anyway.'
'Can I see it think?' I ask.
'You can't see thoughts,' Dad says. 'Don't touch.'
I'm not allowed in Dad's room so I stand quietly, being careful of his beer cans, holding the penknife and the screwdriver for him. Dad's kneeling down. He taps on the outside.
'That's just the casing,' he says.
I can see that.
The back is hard plates with screw holes, and bits of brown tape round the edges because there aren't any screws. Dad cuts the tape with the penknife and pulls out the plates with the screwdriver. It's dark inside and almost empty – it's horrible. Dad pulls out a bit which has little things on it like beans, and a flat bit which he unscrews. I try to pick it up.
'Don't touch!' he says. 'That's the bit that thinks.' He puts it on a sheet of paper. I can't see any thoughts, it isn't any good, so I stamp on it.
Dad shouts, 'Get out! *Out, out, out!*' and he throws the screwdriver at me. It hits my leg and goes right in and blood runs down and fills my shoe.
I run to Mum. She's holding Douggie up against her shoulder, patting his back. Douggie makes a blob of white sick and she wipes it off.
'Don't be such a baby,' she says to me, but she picks me up so Douggie is against one shoulder and I'm against the other. 'It'll soon be time for your Jaffa cake,' she says.
She puts me down but she still holds Douggie. I pinch his toe and run out but he doesn't cry much.
Douggie is new. I was there when Mum cut off his label. He's got dark blue eyes, all misty, and his hair is so thin you can see the plates, like the casing of his head. His skin is even thinner than the tape Dad cut on the computer.
Mum holds Douggie on her knee and smiles at him. Douggie smiles sometimes but not for long, and Mum says it isn't a real smile but it is. Mum looks in his eyes and says: 'I can see what you're thinking, little man, I can see your

thoughts.' She can't with me except when I took a Jaffa cake from the tin, then she could.

'It's written all over your face,' she said. 'I can see it in your eyes,' so she must have seen a Jaffa cake, very small, inside my head.

Piddy isn't allowed in Douggie's room, but sometimes he gets in there even when the door is shut, because he wants to sleep on Douggie. I know how Piddy gets in. I saw him climb the pear tree and when he got as high as Douggie's window he just walked off into the air. He was sort of crawling. I could see his white tummy and I called to him but he didn't look. He went all the way across the garden and in through Douggie's window, there was just his tail. It bent a bit, and went when he jumped.

I told Mum at breakfast.

'What's got into you?' she said. She looked cross but it isn't me who lets Piddy in. 'If you hurt Douggie it won't just be him. You'll feel real bad yourself, you will. Just you remember.'

I go in Dad's room. The penknife and screwdriver are kept in a box down under the window. There's a damp stain like a dragon on the wall, and earwigs live under the box. The penknife is hard to open but I do it and an earwig jumps out onto my hand. It is huge. I drop the knife and run to Mum. She's rocking Douggie because he's been crying a lot.

'Shush,' she says to me. 'Don't be such a baby. Look, Douggie's not crying now, is he?'

I'm not a baby, I'm two. I fetch the penknife and screwdriver and hide them under my bed. I go to see Douggie. He's lying kicking in his basket, it's upside down crawling. I run round and round him, then I stroke his head. His hair is so soft I can hardly feel it but I feel the edges of the plates under his skin. There's a place where I can see the blood going. I put my nose on his nose and look in his eyes. They're red now like Dad's. I can't see any thoughts but they must be in there. I know how to find them. Douggie smells of icecream. He cries and Mum comes and picks him up and tells me to go and play upstairs.

When I come down for my snack Douggie is lying down kicking. He's good at kicking. When he's two I'll give him my shell, I won't want it then. I give him a kiss and put my arms round his head. It's ever so warm. I squeeze and Douggie makes a noise and goes all red.

'You watch it,' Mum says. 'Babies' heads are very delicate, the bones haven't joined up yet. And never touch him here.'

Mum points at the top of Douggie's head, right in the middle. It is so delicate she doesn't even touch. 'The bones haven't joined up here,' she says. I feel my head. I can't find the bit in the middle but my head is very delicate too.

When I go to bed I keep quiet waiting for Douggie to stop crying. I get the penknife and screwdriver and go in. There's always a nightlight on for Douggie, so I can see him. He's sleeping on his back and I try to hear him breathe but I can't. I want the back of his head so I pull him over on his side. He makes a little noise and sucks with his lips, and then he sleeps again.

I shake the penknife in case there's another earwig but there isn't. There's a shiny blue butterfly on Douggie's coat and I cut it off to see how sharp the penknife is. Douggie wakes up and starts the noise he makes before he cries.

'Shush shush shush,' I say, but he doesn't stop. I put my finger in his mouth and he sucks it. His teeth are in there like his thoughts but you can't see them either.

When he's asleep again I kneel down and feel for the plates on the back of his head. With the penknife I make a long cut from near the top, all the way down to his neck. He can't feel it because he's asleep. Then I make two cuts across, and push the screwdriver in to get the plates open.

I look in. It's all dark in there, and empty, even emptier than Dad's computer. There are no thoughts, there aren't even any dreams. Right through on the front bit two lighter patches show, like the little windows in my room when the curtains are shut and it's light outside. They are Douggie's eyes. I can't see through because they are shut.

In the morning I look in Douggie's eyes. Right in the middle of each one there's a real window, round like the windows on my picture of a boat. It's dark in there but I see one of his thoughts. It's white and sliding about. It's a nappy. I go to tell Mum and she runs in to see if Douggie's all right. But he is, of course he is. She picks him up and looks in his eyes and forgets about me.

I go in Dad's room and pull the toolbox away from the

wall. There's an earwig sitting on the dragon's eye. It isn't the one that chased me before, but another, smaller one, but it's a proper earwig. I catch it in the matchbox where I keep my shell.

I lie in my bed waiting for Douggie to stop crying like a baby. I kick my feet and wait and wait. There's a bit of light on the ceiling like a thin face. I shut my eyes and watch a story. When Douggie stops crying I go in. This time it is easy to cut open his head, and I don't even need the screwdriver, the plates open like doors. I put the earwig in there by shaking it out of the matchbox so it doesn't touch me, and shut the doors quickly. Mum hates earwigs too. When she looks into Douggie's eyes in the morning she's going to have a fright.

In the middle of the night I wake up and hear a noise from Douggie's room. I go to look. He is sitting up in his basket with his eyes open.

'It's night time, you must lie down,' I say. I pull down his lip and he smiles. 'You're my brother,' I whisper.

I go behind him to look at the earwig. I open the doors a tiny bit and suddenly they push wide open. Douggie's head is full, full of earwigs, all piled up and sliding down in heaps, and they all tumble out on me and run inside my pyjamas and down my tummy and legs and up my arms and neck and in my ears. I scream and scream and scream until Mum comes.

James Cressey

URCHIN

In rural Perthshire, in the centre of Scotland, where I grew up hedgehogs or 'urchins' had a mixed reputation. My father, a farm labourer, maintained that they sucked the milk from cows lying out in the pasture at night and he killed them on sight. He then fixed the skins to gateposts to prevent cattle rubbing themselves against them – it did less damage than barbed-wire. My mother thought that they were unlucky and, if one stumbled into the house, shouted for my father to kill it.

In the fields I noticed that, despite their excellent natural protection, they had other predators. A determined badger or fox would roll them into a burn or pond and attack them when, uncurled, they swam onto the bank.

Grannie, who was very proud of her gypsy ancestry, said that not only were they pleasant to eat but that they could cure the 'fits'. Once when I was feverish and the local doctor too pissed to move Grannie made a hedgehog pie – you cover it in clay, bake it in the oven, and the prickly skin detaches with the hardened earth. But the idea of eating the wretched animal was so nauseous that I recovered immediately. I liked the little beasts and carefully removed from harm any that I found.

When my father died an unpleasant death under a harvesting machine ('The urchins' revenge,' muttered Grannie) my mother and I went down to stay with her parents in Edinburgh. My mother, who was intermittently capable of making the right decision, left my father's mother behind.

It was difficult for me to get work in Edinburgh: I'd missed a lot of schooling during the busy seasons on the farm and I had a thick accent laden with dialect. Eventually, however, I got a job as an animal house attendant; they at least liked the fact that I'd worked on a farm. And it was here that, once again, hedgehogs entered my life.

The laboratory was researching, among other pests, certain ticks. I cannot remember what they were called although they had a name as fine as their coloured camouflage.

When the hedgehogs arrived – supplied by a farm-hand sharper than my father had been – we sprayed them with mild disinfectant from 'atomisers' – this killed their normal parasites. The creatures were then hosed down and, when they'd dried out, the researchers placed on them the ticks that they were interested in.

The hedgehogs were fed on meaty cat food and milk – my father may have been right about that – and, sometimes, as a special treat, live cockroaches were brought down from the insect rooms. They seemed content and were, with time, friendly, but Christ did they smell. They occasionally bred in captivity and it was curious to see the young piglets, blind and helpless, but already armed with quills that would soon harden. The Chief Technician had taken a couple home and said they kept his garden free of slugs, insects and vermin.

I liked to go along to the aquarium and see the strange animals there: timid octopi; sea-anemones, sensitive, beautiful, but ruthless in the kill; and, of course, sea-urchins. Charles, the aquarium technician, who'd been expelled from public school, did a nice line in paper-weights made from the shells of dead sea-urchins. These brightly coloured tests, filled with sand, could be seen on desks all through the laboratory. I thought that they looked nicer alive and for my few pieces of paper used an old horse-shoe that Dad had kept – not that it had done him much good, poor sod. Charles said that he'd been told in school that the ancient Greeks had used the shells of sea-urchins for a jury's voting pot. But he'd tell you any bloody story just to stand close to you and put his hand with those long nails on your shoulder.

Meantime I was going to evening classes to improve my English and there I met Luciana. Perhaps what attracted me to her was that she was as prickly as any urchin, though given that she was a big girl my private nick-name for her was 'The Porcupine'. She was touchy first about her bad English and then because she was Italian and had encountered people for whom that damn war will never be over.

Anyway we got talking. Initially we talked about superstitions. Italians are a very superstitious nation. I told her about hedgehogs and she'd come up with interesting facts like that thirteen is generally a lucky number in Italy and that the really bad day is Tuesday the seventeenth. So we fell in love, which requires little conversation, and when our English had improved enough we got through the formalities of betrothal and marriage.

Then her father had one of those vague yet mandatory summonses that happen in Italian families and all of them – with me – went back to Rome. So here was another language to learn.

There wasn't much for me to do in the family business so mostly I watched the sport on TV. The people were fine and the food OK though I hated it when anybody in a restaurant ordered octopus – I'd remember them diffident and graceful in the crepuscular aquarium.

As the years passed and Luciana and I had no children my father-in-law came to suspect that there might be something lacking in my masculinity. One day, in autumn, I got a call to meet him at a swish restaurant off Via Veneto. We were surrounded by people at the other tables who spoke English with thicker accents than I had started out with – Americans who constantly asked the waiter to bring a telephone to their table.

As a starter, casually, hoping that I would not understand the Italian, my father-in-law ordered the gonads of sea-urchins. Long ago in Edinburgh, in an aquarium, surrounded by an earlier and cleaner world, Charles had told me that Italians considered this dish an aphrodisiac.

When I was left with the ice-cream and Strega, my father-in-law having gone to another appointment, I went into the toilet and made myself sick by thrusting my fingers down my throat. I remembered that Charles had said that the ancient Romans did this, though I think they used a feather.

Afterwards I decided to walk across the Villa Borghese and see the animals in the zoo. Near one of the main paths was a huge horse-chestnut tree and I found myself treading on the countless empty shells – the kids had taken the conkers. Flattened on the damp earth they looked like squashed baby hedgehogs.

Recoiling, I sat down on a bench, and wept for the urchin.

Alexander J. Cuthbert

THE IMPOSSIBILITY OF PURE WATER

The glass of water rests on the table
beside me with all the light in the room
pouring into it.   Lifting the glass to
my mouth I feel the surface tense against
my top lip, and through my fish eye
the colours of the room form rings inside
each other, telescoping into the tiny
bubble trapped between the stem and bowl.

The glass appears impossibly over-
full like that of Velazquez's *Water
Seller*, who passes the unsullied
Eucharist from one generation to
the next — the fabled gift of pure water.

The secret of catching transparency
is about not painting that which is not
there, it's about showing the unfocused,
imprecision and vagueness of our vision.

Iain Crichton Smith saw it and claimed, in
his driest island schoolmaster's voice, that
'the fact of water is unteachable,'
as if purity and poverty were
opposites, as if somehow the poorest
man would be unable to find the purest
water.   Yet it is common knowledge, to
those close enough to the edges to hear,
that only after the climb above the
highest summer grazing, or a stumble
across a spring issuing freely from
deep beneath ground, that the fact of water
can be held up to the eye of the sun,
before tasting the difference it holds.

Water has memory. Chemists agree
that traces persist to be recorded
long after the negative integers
of dilution prove that they have gone.
Nothing is lost to water. It holds all.

Water has memory. Seven times it
passes through seven different city
dwellers before it finally reaches
the sea. Each time something connects, between
vegetable, animal and human –
the chain grows. Nothing is lost to water.

Some fear death by water, the drowning of
the still small voice by the monopoly
of violence that searches for sources while
leaving the surface uncovered, stagnant.

Those who have drunk tainted water
take it personally, it's an offence
like no other, part shock – part disgust, then
self-loathing at the sudden impulse to
keep drinking, to keep on going despite the
taste of flesh and straw.
                       You feel like a dog
lapping at a toilet bowl, but the wetness,
the coolness of it makes you want to
forget that you have just seen the carcass
now six feet upstream from your cupped hands.

I break the silence of the room inside
the glass and release the extra sip that
the surface tension held in place – and then
the possibility of pure water is lost forever
as I catch my own reflection flickering through
the draining light.
                Like Carracci's *Man Drinking*, I stare
upward through the bottom of the misting globe,

poised as if something had just happened,
as if a hole had opened in the sky.

If I could breathe for long enough the glass
would refill and I might begin again,
but every taste is unrepeatable;
every drink of water an end in itself:
it reflects all we can see and it holds
all we are, making us thirst as we drink.

Vicki Feaver

SLOES

He was in Paris for the weekend:
on his own — you were mad
to think otherwise.

You took the children
on an expedition with friends
to pick sloes — small bitter plums
from the spiky twigs
of the blackthorn; best picked
after the first frosts
have loosened the stones.

Your friends were going to soak them in gin
ready for Christmas.

You couldn't think that far.
You couldn't even think
as far as next weekend;
or the stallion, black as a sloe,
galloping above you
down a sloping field.

GREEN

Whatever she gave him
he looked disappointed,
as if he were thinking
if you really loved me
you'd know what I wanted.

Then, one Christmas,
she bought him a philodendron
and he seemed to be pleased.
From then on she decided
always to give him a plant.

His room filled up with pots.
She stopped going in there
as if all that green
had somehow replaced her.
'It's like a jungle,' friends exclaimed

and they brought him
ailing cacti and ferns
to nurse back to health.
Fingers that pushed her roughly away
touched leaves tenderly.

He was kind to plants
she vowed to have chiselled
on his grave – not knowing
that a couple of streets away
another woman bloomed.

Graham Fulton

REMAINDERS
In memory of my cat Fay, 1984–2001

While scooting about with the hoover gadget
a tiny whiteness attracts my eye.
I stoop to lift a single whisker
stuck at the foot of the skirting board
beneath the window, in the lounge.
My little cat. Dead two years
after living for sixteen years.

All this time, avoiding the housework.
Hiding at the carpet edge
among the crumbs, the skin and fluff,
occasional crispies and shrivelled peas.
Remainders that we never see.
Reminders we are less than perfect,
less than the sum of what we believe.

A finely tapering thread of thin,
slightly, between my finger and thumb.
It brings it back. The things we let slip
as life cleans up. Baffling love
for something with a raisin-sized brain.
Instinct signals. Redundant words.
A bell round her neck to warn the birds.

It'll go in the box that held her ash,
along with her name tag, shred of claw,
silverfoil-ball she was born to chase.
Essential, sentimental guff.
Resistance against the unforgiving
sweeping away of everything
that's ever been, will never be.

THIS IS YOUR LIFE

A red volume, full of pictures,
on your dressing table stool.
We put it together for your birthday.
70, 1999.

All your life, or what we could find.
Baby in pram, girl to woman,
work, pals, wedding romance.
Images of your mother and father.
Images of the children you had.

Hugging us safe inside your coat
after we came back from our gran's.
Winter Sundays, waiting for dad
to catch a fire, shovel the ashes,
match the twisted papers and coals.
Toasting bread on a long-pronged fork,
showing us nothing is under the bed.

We gave you the book.
You went out dancing.
Came back home, plugged in the fire,
wore an I AM 70 badge.

Now you're a name on a cemetery plaque,
an image fixed to a cloister wall.
Yet what remains is so much more
than 6 by 4's in a ringbound token,
bags of Get Well, Sympathy cards,
bills and scraps in a chest of drawers.

It's easy to smile when you reach my mind.
I see you walking along the street,
singing a past-times song to yourself,
concentrating on watching your feet,
useful advice to keep from falling.
Something your granny used to believe,
something her granny used to believe.

It's all true. You'll always be.
Unfallen, warm, inside us, safe.
This beat, then this beat.

rab swannock fulton

ahm grinnin lik an eejit

ahm grinnin lik an eejit
when yi step inside
ahm itchin fae wurds n nonwurds
jaggin mi skin
wae cardomon
n banana slices stewin
ahv gote hunnurs ah waant tae say
but cin ainly brek haets fae thi cosmic
send thum whizzin thur peerie-wee waye tae yi
wurds
aboot lovin yae missin yae
n thi currys nearly ready

Robin Fulton

OCTET

Eight backs to the rain in a ring beneath
a sycamore, backs to the streaming crowd,
eight saxophonists play eight saxophones.
The rain can't stop. The crowd won't stop. The dead
who have time to stop and listen I hope
are delighted. I stop. For days I hear
eight glowing tigers showing they have learnt
to growl softly and contrapuntally.

THE RIVER HELMSDALE

Such confidence in the sound of its voice
– the river can keep one statement going
day and night for centuries. No question
ever. We can listen or we can leave.

I left but I still hear the surface rush
that disguises the depth of the Coach Pool
just up from Telford's bridge, especially
at low tide. When the river has spread out

and vanished into the wide Moray Firth
no-one could see from high in a plane or
low in a boat which molecules had poured
with the overflow from Loch an Ruathair

and which had dripped gently from pool to pool
of the hesitant burn at Kilphedir.
There is much distress waiting for rivers
who believe in water and nothing but.

GEOGRAPHY LESSONS

I

Miniature Kent and Essex parting
as the Thames becomes sea not river.

A window minding its own business,
at the wrong angle for me, cobalt

now then dipping to estuaries
on that live map whose scale is shrinking:

Blackwater, Stour and Orwell. The last
I see of land is the Alde's right-turn

just short of where it might touch the sea,
its thin miles southwards along the shore.

II

Five and a half degrees east, same day,
I am miniature, life-sized beneath

a pine tree, it too minding its own
business, its decades stacked on one spot.

The uneventfulness of its growth
is my invention. I give it, too,

a magnetic field of loneliness
with which it slows my steps then stops them.

I stare at the bark close-up: it's rough
mountain terrain glimpsed from cruising height.

Iain Galbraith

BLUE WINGS

Return to base was a glide by dawn,
hips kissing across the sheets of ice.

Clacking fieldfares packed the orange grass.
And then the sea! The sea, its rose epithelium

scuffed and torn, sported a tanker that slipped
off the edge, flaming at two degrees.

Back in the bay the hooks and pulleys
guaranteed a curtain and the shifting sand

a jetsam theatre, its blue wings propped
by driftwood boughs. For all the miles

of foreshore scanned from the air they found
only two men fishing from the head.

No mistaking the stars' pinpointed scrawl.
No knowing what the actors will say

when the tall waves climb the marbled quay
and the haven faints, just beyond recall.

Mark Gallacher

THE MILES

Only hours before Robert Connell walked out of his old life forever, some students, Robert's daughter Elaine among them, tumbled out of the exam hall into the clear sunshine, like bright confetti scuffed in a breeze.

When Wallace came down the steps onto the street he avoided the other students and leaned against a lamp post. In his pocket a present wrapped in silver paper, tied in blue ribbon.

His heart hammered in his chest. It was only a dumb present but his stupid body hadn't caught up with the idea, lacked nerve. He rolled his exam paper into a tube to give his hands something to do and waited for Elaine to break away from her girl friends.

Breezy girl talk fluttered back and forth in the breathless air. A flurry of postures rippled around the group: hair pulled back, the swishing of skirts. A riot of perfumes dousing the senses.

At last Elaine turned from her friends. Wallace walked up to her and gave her the present. 'Well done. Glasgow University beckons.'

'Thanks,' she said, but didn't open the present. 'Phew! It was a bugger. I didn't think I'd have enough time.'

Two of Elaine's friends suddenly dragged her away. Wallace resented it. It wasn't going as he'd planned. He felt undermined. There wasn't anybody left around he wanted to make small talk with. Mostly the cleverer students, discussing the merits of their answers, worrying over stuff Wallace hadn't even thought of, which made him lightheaded with panic.

Elaine had walked off with her friends and incredibly, she wasn't going to open the present or even say goodbye. Worse still, Wallace was following them.

Elaine said something to her friends and turned around. She walked back to Wallace. 'I have to go with this lot. Drinks at Marie's house,' she said. She came closer, more intimate, her eyes coy and bright. 'The present was sweet. But you –'

Wallace tried to kiss her. Elaine laughed and pushed

him away. 'My lipstick, you idiot! Honestly.' Now she was annoyed. Her friends told her to hurry up. 'Have to go,' she said, and hurried off.

'What about the dance tonight?' Wallace called after her. 'Remember? Pick you up at seven?'

'What?' Elaine acted as if she hadn't heard. 'Oh. Come around half past eight. If you really want to.'

The Connell family house was built on raised ground on the western edge of the town, overlooking the golf course and the slate-blue sea beyond. A house with small windows and sandstone walls. A house that had too much shade in summer, too little light in winter, so that it always seemed a cold place, with no garden to redeem it.

Robert Connell came into the thin hallway of the house after his twelve-hour shift at the distillery. He hung his coat on the hook. Saw his reflection in the long mirror. A tired man with grey hair. His tall reedy body already trying out the postures of old age.

Robert walked into the kitchen. His wife and daughter were already eating their dinner. Elaine had her bathrobe on, wet towel wrapped around her head. She rubbed moisturising cream into her hands.

'What's that?' Robert pointed at a plain gold necklace on the table, some crumpled gift paper next to it.

Elaine laughed. 'It's *so* cheap and tacky, Dad. Wallace Croft gave me it after the exam today. I dated him a couple of times this month.'

Robert sat down. 'Billy Croft's a fisherman. Not a lot of money in that house.'

'Oh really, Robert! Don't start moralising now.' Elaine's mother cut at the meat on her plate. 'And you haven't taken your boots off. Again. I can smell the distillery on you.'

'I'll go up and change then.'

'That's right.'

Robert left the kitchen but hovered near the door and listened to them talk. He was fifty years old. His wife Elizabeth was forty-seven, looked younger. His daughter would start university after the summer. She was going to study Fine Art.

'Richard Thompson is picking me up at seven, Mum.

I'm going to the dance with him. He's got a car. And not one of those rusty wrecks the others drive around town in. A Ford Fusion. I'll date him for the rest of the summer. Then I'll dump him.' Elaine giggled at her own ruthlessness.

'Why will you dump him at the end of the summer?'

'Oh Mum. I can't go to university with a boyfriend from around here. That's so small town stuff. I'll shop around in Glasgow.'

'There'll be plenty of candidates, I'm sure,' Elizabeth said approvingly. Then she raised her voice. 'Robert, are you dithering in the hallway listening to us talking?'

A conspiratorial silence fell across the house. Robert took his boots off, sat them down at the front door. He walked upstairs. He stripped in the bedroom, put his work clothes in the laundry basket and went into the bathroom and showered.

Robert thought about his mother, their last conversation in the retirement home. His mother had shrunk in those last months; become small and hollow, as if she'd contained the small bones of birds. She didn't eat much more than buttered bread, mashed vegetables, watery warm soup. But her mind was sharp, her temper brittle.

'I've left the money to you,' she told him and yawned and fell asleep. She woke up again ten minutes later and carried on the conversation.

'I haven't left anything for Malcolm. He's enough money of his own. Anyway, his ex-wives would only take it all. And Elizabeth won't get a penny of it. Promise me.'

'She's my wife,' Robert said weakly.

'She's no daughter of mine,' his mother snapped. 'And she's been no kind of wife to you! If you give her any of your inheritance then you will have wasted mine and your father's good intentions. Why do you think she's never visited me here? Because she thinks I've no money. There's no reward in it for her. And you can forget about Elaine. She's got all her mother's vanities and weaknesses. Not one good trait from our side of the family.'

'You're being hard. You don't know what you're saying.'

'Robert. Robert. I know what I'm saying and I say it because I love you. I've hopes for you yet, son.' She sniffed on a handkerchief and then she fell asleep again.

Robert waited and just when he thought his mother would not wake up again, her dry dusty breath whistling in her sunken mouth, she suddenly smiled with her eyes closed. 'You were such a curious boy! Eyes open to the world. Now stop talking and let me sleep.'

The funeral had been a month ago. His brother Malcolm had flown back from Toronto. Malcolm was thirty years old, owned a restaurant and a successful Scottish theme bar called The Big Man. Malcolm was fit and healthy, a sportsman's strut to his stride, with an amused light in those brown eyes that were quick to flash impatience.

Malcolm had arrived with a young woman no-one had met before. Her name was Patricia. She was small and pretty and spoke with a hushed, painfully polite voice. After the funeral service Malcolm drove her to a hotel and came back to Robert's house. Elizabeth had arranged tea and sandwiches.

At the house Malcolm flirted openly with all the women, even his niece. Elizabeth watched him warily every time he came near Elaine.

Robert asked timidly if Patricia was a serious girlfriend. 'God no,' Malcolm answered. 'Only met her a week ago. Fantastic body on her. Don't you think?'

Elizabeth put fresh sandwiches on the table. 'How can you bring a stranger to your own mother's funeral?'

Malcolm laughed. 'I'm sure Mum doesn't approve. But she always said you had to live life. Not worry about it. Isn't that right, Robert? Anyway, when I see her in heaven she can give me a ticking off.'

Elizabeth crossed her arms. 'How can you believe in heaven when you're such a sinner?'

Malcolm lifted a glass of wine. 'That's easy. You just have to be Catholic.'

After the wine was finished and only a few of the mourners remained, Malcolm insisted that Robert come with him to the pub. It would be their wake. Elizabeth agreed to it, relieved to get Malcolm out of the house, away from Elaine's thrilled eyes.

The two brothers walked down to the pub in the cool evening. Malcolm sighed, disappointed by how little the town had changed. Then he suddenly changed subject and gripped Robert's arm. Robert was faintly embarrassed by his younger brother's sudden seriousness.

'I know she left you the money,' Malcolm said quietly. 'I'm okay with that. With all my heart I mean it. Just promise me you'll think about what you'll do with it. It could be your last chance.'

In the Harbour Bar people greeted Malcolm cheerily, offered condolences. Robert ordered beer while Malcolm asked for the best whisky in the house.

Robert went back downstairs to the kitchen to eat his dinner, while Elizabeth filled the dishwasher. Elaine had gone to her room to finish changing.

'Have you heard from your no-good brother since the funeral?'

Robert fiddled with the gold necklace. Thought about all the jewellery he had bought down the years. There had to be miles of it in her jewellery box. 'No.'

'I didn't think so. He's so selfish, that man. Only ever thinking about himself. If you hurry up with your dinner I can start the dishwasher.'

Robert looked up. 'Are you worried we'll be all right after Elaine's gone off to the university? What do they call it now. Empty Nest Syndrome.'

'Here. Give me that.' Elizabeth took the necklace from Robert, threw it in the bin. 'I'll be visiting her often enough. Then there's her flat. We have to get that organised. I don't want her staying in some awful student halls of residence. There's lots to do. She'll need new clothes. Things for the flat. You can't say no to any overtime at the distillery. Even Sundays. We need the money.'

The front doorbell rang and Elaine swept downstairs. 'I'm going!' she shouted. 'Don't wait up for me. I'm a big girl now.'

Laughter echoed in the hallway. The hard muscular voice of a young man. Elizabeth left the kitchen. When she came back Robert had placed his empty plate and glass in the dishwasher.

'I'm going upstairs for a bath,' she said, wiping the kitchen table one last time.

Robert sat back down.

'What's wrong with you?'

'Nothing.'

Elizabeth narrowed her eyes. 'Really, Robert, I've no

patience for you when you're like this. You've been moping around the house for weeks. Get your act together.'

Elizabeth went upstairs for her bath. Robert found a newspaper, switched the radio on. He lost track of time, only half reading the newspaper. Something about the new Parliament building costing a fortune, and house prices in Edinburgh going through the roof. There was a photograph of the new Parliament building site, what looked like cranes and scaffolding, odd architectural shapes like upturned boats, or giant steel clams. Robert hoped the place might at least be something beautiful to visit.

The doorbell rang. Robert walked down the hallway and opened the front door. Wallace stood there on the porch, in his best clothes, aftershave that could cut steel.

'She's gone already. I'm sorry,' Robert told the boy.

Wallace stepped back, looked off into the distance.

Elizabeth shouted from upstairs. 'If that's the Croft boy tell him Elaine doesn't want to see him any more. And he mustn't bother her!'

Robert started to apologise again but Wallace only shook his head and walked away.

Robert went back into the kitchen. He sat down and looked at his hands. Lumpy long-fingered creatures, the skin leathered with years of work. His wedding ring impossibly shiny against the dull yellowed flesh.

Robert walked over to the rubbish bin, took the necklace out and studied it. He rolled the necklace up and put it in his pocket. He lifted the rubbish bag from the bin and tied a knot in it. He carried it into the hallway. Put his jacket on.

It was a fine warm evening outside. The bottle-green sea unravelled lazy waves along the tide line. Arran lay vividly lit in the west; a last flowering of sunshine cascaded across the peak of Goat Fell. In front of the island flakes of sunlight burned like pieces of gold leaf scattered across the water.

Robert put the rubbish in the bin by the side of the road and walked onto the golf course. He breathed in the cool sea air. He noticed a boy sat on a bench nearby, guessed it was Wallace.

Robert walked over and sat down. Wallace was drinking beer, smoking a cigarette.

'I don't get it,' Wallace muttered.

Robert asked for a beer and Wallace gave him a can. Robert sighed, opened the can and took a long drink. He found the necklace in his pocket. 'Here,' he said, and gave it to Wallace.

'Thanks. Don't know what I'll do with it though.'

Robert nodded. 'Listen,' he said. 'I'm going to tell you something. My wife and daughter aren't nice people. My wife – well, I don't think she's loved anyone in a long time. My daughter is shallow and spoiled. I'm sorry she's treated you so badly.'

Wallace's mouth fell open.

'Will you not go to the dance?' Robert asked and smiled.

'I don't know.'

'You should go. There are other girls. After the summer you may never come back to the town. You want to take good memories with you.'

'I don't know.'

'Well.' Robert stood up. 'Don't dwell on it for too long. That just leads to indecision. I have to go.'

'Goodbye, Mr Connell.'

'Goodbye, Wallace.'

Robert wandered back to the house, but felt a need to walk down to the beach. He cut across the golf course and stood on the sand and looked out at the waves. He picked up a pebble, weighed it in his hand, faintly self-conscious of the symbolism, threw it in.

When he finally came back to the house Elizabeth had already gone to bed, all the downstairs lights turned off. The dishwasher thrummed in the kitchen. He stood in the hallway and listened to the small sounds of the house.

Elizabeth was in bed reading when Robert came into the room. Her face was covered in night cream, her dark hair on her thin shoulders like straw. She smelled of antiseptic.

'Elizabeth.'

'What is it *now*?'

'We have to start again, Elizabeth. We have to start over. The whole thing.'

'Don't be a bloody fool, Robert!' she hissed, and her face curled up into a grotesque callous mask. The hatred in her voice stunned them both.

Elizabeth blinked up at him, hesitated, but then she

closed her heart to pity. She slammed the book shut. 'I'm sick and tired of this stupidity! Ever since the funeral. If you're not coming to bed then go downstairs and watch television. Do something!'

Elizabeth rolled over. She switched off the light and pulled the blanket up to her chin. Robert hovered in the darkness. He turned and walked out of the room and shut the door quietly behind him.

Robert left the house and opened the boot of the car. There was a small holdall there and he opened it. Some clothes. Some travel books. His passport.

He locked the boot and sat in the car, put the keys in the ignition, took the handbrake off. The car rolled quietly down the driveway and he turned it onto the road and then he started the engine and drove away.

Robert circled the town for a while in the deepening dusk. He drove down the High Street a last time and turned onto the road that passed the school. He saw the exam hall lit up, the end of term dance started. The front of the hall was decorated with posters and balloons.

Robert saw Wallace just ahead. He slowed the car to a stop on the other side of the road.

Wallace hesitated outside the hall. The doors were open and neon disco light pulsed weakly in the otherwise impenetrable darkness of the doorway. A doorman said something to Wallace. The boy walked up the steps and handed his ticket over.

Robert held his breath. Wallace paused again. Robert willed him to go inside. He had to go inside because the heart could not be turned back. The hope of love was no sin, even if those on the other side had burned up their own measure of it. Even if they waited with cold indifference and the ashes of their smiles.

Finally Wallace walked inside.

Robert drove onto the coast road. He drove past the distillery and kept going. He did not know where he was going. Tears welled in his eyes and he wiped them away with the back of his hand. He couldn't be certain if it was grief for his mother or his own lost life. He switched the radio on. But there was no music that could match his longing or his loneliness.

When the man walked into the bar some of the customers looked up, saw a family likeness in the still features of his face. Malcolm was talking on the phone. He put the phone down and came out from behind the bar.

'I can only stay a minute,' Robert explained. 'I don't want to get a ticket.'

Malcolm nodded. 'Back in a minute folks.' Malcolm pointed to a man in a hunting jacket at the bar. 'Don't you try and pour a free one while I'm outside.'

The two brothers walked outside and stood by the car. 'Jesus, Robert! You did it. Jesus. You didn't kill her, did you?'

Robert smiled. 'Which one?'

Malcolm laughed, shook his head. 'It's too much to take in. Which way are you heading? What will you do with yourself?'

'I'm heading north. See the lakes and the mountains.' Robert sat back in the car. 'I'll come visit. On the way back. I promise.'

'Sure. Sure.' Malcolm leaned down. 'I mean you bloody better!' He laughed and slapped the roof of the car. 'But listen. Now listen, it's bloody cold up there.'

'I like north. Less people.' Robert started the car. 'Take care of yourself, Malcolm.'

'You too. You too.'

Malcolm watched the car vanish in the traffic. He looked up and down the street, not sure what to do with himself. He spun on his heels and ran back into the bar.

Paul Gorman

A SWARMING

Yes. We knew the beekeeper. We knew of him, that is. We saw him often that summer, walking along the edge of our football field. He would have a hat with a veil in one hand, and from the other swung a holdall. Its momentum pulled him along in jolts, like a slow train. The long grass stems whipped against his shins. We never spoke to him. To begin with.

The adults didn't know him. Mention *the beekeeper* or *the hives* and in their bewilderment the blank grown-up faces became briefly readable. We began to wonder if he existed only for us, if he was something no-one else was aware of. Something secret that belonged to us. That he was ours.

Yes, we actually watched him at the hives sometimes. He was visible, even through the trees. We'd stand, or crouch, hawthorns pricking our skin in the cool thicket while the hot air of late afternoon throbbed with bees. He lifted these wooden frames out of the hive, one after another, all heavy with wax, and everything he did was in slow motion, like a cosmonaut. The thick sunlight caught the bees' wings and it was like dry, golden rain. We remember that.

It was Tom he spoke to first. Tom was small, quiet, unthreatening: perhaps that was the reason, we never found out. But he began talking to Tom, being friendly, only Tom didn't tell us. At first, we didn't know. Tom was one of us: there was no reason to suspect. One day though he passed us, close-by – the beekeeper – and greeted Tom. Said 'hello' or something, called him by name. That shut us up; that got us wondering. We kept our mouths shut for a bit, and our eyes open.

Yes, he'd shown Tom the inside of the hives. The guts. We wondered when this had happened. When had Tom spent so much time away, with the beekeeper? The man gave him the use of a veil, and even the little tin that puffed smoke. It made the bees drowsy, Tom said. The man showed him the eggs that the new bees would hatch from, and the honey, capped over with wax in tight little pockets. Tom told us all of this, but it was like it wasn't Tom, just a little version of a grown-up, squawking all these phrases like a puppet. And so the harder we asked him, the more he told us. Even the man's name.

He was scared, the first time we called him by name. We could see that. Adults might lie with more skill than children, but their faces don't. We were encouraged, but we didn't let it show. And slowly, week by week, he softened like the beeswax he gave us, rubbed between warm fingers. He relaxed when we were around. And we asked him questions, like model pupils. We learned about bees.

Everything had to be done slowly, so as not to alarm the bees. He turned the frames over, pointed out this or that feature, or some oddity of behaviour. The little immaculate rows of hexagonal cells. The different compartments of the hive, as distinct as the three parts of an insect: head, thorax, abdomen. He explained the way the bees order themselves – how each bee, depending on age or breed, has a specific job and how all of the jobs fitted together neatly like the cells of honey, for the good of the hive. All very interesting, and we soaked it up, like bread. We noticed the half-bricks that raised the hives above the level of the ground, and the basin of water with a towel draped over it from which the bees could drink. We took it all in. It was our project.

But his favourite was Tom. It was obvious. Tom would hold the smoker, and under instruction and a guiding hand would use it to pacify the insects. Tom would scrape a palette knife of honey with trembling gloved hands. The bees flew in his face like a nuisance little brother. The motion of them made us sick. Blinking away, everything in sight crawling and writhing with the hum of their wings thick in our heads like pollen. But Tom, immune, saw and heard nothing of this. He was lost to us.

It took only a few words, carefully chosen, to weave the beekeeper into existence for the adults, and only a few more to embroider a picture of where he stood between us and Tom. Words have a power greater than those who use them.

When they told us that Tom had run away, we knew it was only his starting point on the journey back to us. He would return, he would be found.

He was found two days later, on the shore of the loch.

It was raining, we remember that. It was raining when

we started to cry. It was still raining when we lifted off the felt roof of the hives and emptied the basin of water inside. It was raining, and the soles of our trainers slipped and squeaked as we kicked them over and they splintered open. The raw wood, red like exposed skin, darkened in the rain. And when the beekeeper appeared we were ready for him. The trees were strong and the branches hard to break, but now as we hold them in our sweating hands we fill our lungs with tree dust and we smell like men.

He stumbled over the half bricks and we hit him in the face. Head, thorax, abdomen. It surprised us how easily he went down, with a noise like the cracking of the hives. Like an echo; again and again and again.

There was so much silence afterwards: the blood was thick in our ears and we couldn't hear the bees. So much silence, like it was a heavy weight. Like when something is crushed under a thumb or heel and breaks into shards, with broken edges and splinters in between that scatter and vanish so it can never be put together again. I remember that.

Rody Gorman

FRANK O'HARA: DÀN

Siud Frank O'Hara
'S e a' falbh gu lòn
Air a' bhliadhna san d'rugadh mi fhìn
'S a' dèanamh dàin
Mu bhith falbh gu lòn
'S a' dèanamh dàin
Air a' bhliadhna
San d'rugadh mi fhìn.

Am-bliadhna,
Seo mi fhìn
A' falbh gu lòn 's a' dèanamh dàin
Mu Frank O'Hara
'S e a' falbh gu lòn 's a' dèanamh dàin
Mu bhith falbh gu lòn
'S a' dèanamh dàin
Air a' bhliadhna san d'rugadh mi fhìn.

CUILEAG-SHNEACHDA

Leig mi 'n uinneag mu sgaoil sa mhadainn
Ach am beanadh an tè bhàn
Ri sneachda den chiad turas
Agus, mar bu dual,
'S ann a chuir e iongnadh oirre,
Iongnadh mòr an t-saoghail.

'S e th' innte gun teagamh
Cuileag-shneachda, na dealbh air leth
Nach robh a h-aon samhail cruinn ann a-riamh
An dèidh gun tèid an gnè air ais gu tùs na cruinne
'S a mhaireas dreis
Is nach tig am follais a thuilleadh.

DÌREACH GUS A RÀDH

Chuir mi crìoch
Air an *Tè Bheag*
A dh'fhàg
Thu air a' bhòrd

Is a chuir thu an taobh,
Tha fios, a dh'aon steall
Airson a' chèilidh a-nochd.

Tha mi duilich:
Bha i eireachdail.
Rinn i feum dhomh.

GLUASAD

Air chuairt an-diugh sa mhol,
Dh'fhidir mi bhuam aitealach
Ris a' ghruaigean le corran-caol
Is cliabh aig ìsle-làin,
A' gluasad air èiginn.

Chan eil mi 'g ràdh
Nach biodh i fhìn air aon
De na *Haenyeo*
A b' fheàrr a bh' ann an Eilean Udo
Riamh roimhe na linn.

SHINGLE

Out walking today on the shingle,
I saw a cailleach collecting seaweed with a knife
and creel, the tide almost out,
hardly moving at all.

For all I know, she might
have been one of the finest Haenyeo
ever on the island of Udo
back when she was a girl.

Charlie Gracie

rain

sometimes the rain spears the light into cold glass
stretches its fingers about your shoulders
soddens every last inch of you

sometimes it smudges the edges of the day
floats like dust on your jumper and your hair
simmers on your skin in a cool fizz

when it's not here
it is likely somewhere else
colouring the buildings in Paisley
spattering dog shite in the High Street in Buckie
swirling grey in Peebles like an old woman's hair

and even when the sunshine bakes us
the rain is only hiding
smirring off the surface of the sea
gathering its breath
for the big Heave Ho

Rosemary Hector

BRENT MILLAR'S LOVEBIRDS

So I says to her 'the point is
do you add, or take from?
In making things, I mean –
songs, stories, puddings –
the question's the same.
Is it "less is more",
or does more make it better?'
She says she don't know, but
sometimes there's nothing left
to take from, and other times
adding seems superfluous.
So there we are, on the branch,
me all superior, like,
and her looking quite demure
as if she'd fly only if pushed.
(I'd dare not try; her staying here's
always been optional.)
And the pastel of her blush
is mine now and we've added
and been taken from
by more than offspring.
We even share the stroke
of the artist's hand
as he's swept across our breasts.
All pink – both of us
and green above us – the same load
of colour all in one.
'But then' she says
'What's the point in talking
of adding or taking?
We're one and I add
what you take and
you add what I take and
the question is only about
making, and we've already
made and made and made
and that's more than we
can talk about tonight, my love.'

Kate Hendry

ALL THAT GLASS

She told me she didn't want to sleep in our bedroom any more. I thought she meant in our bed, with me. So I offered to move out. 'If you want,' I ventured, 'I'll sleep in the spare room.' I thought it was up to me to make things right. 'Your choice,' she replied, sounding surprised, 'but I'm moving into the conservatory. You can come too, if you like, or stay put, or try the spare room. I'm not bothered.'

Three rooms to choose from. In fact, I got the feeling she wouldn't have minded if I'd moved in with Timmy. Or into the bathroom. She never used it these days anyway. She might have minded if I'd set myself up in the kitchen. But there's no room left in there and I'm not one to make a point. 'I'll come with you, if that's okay,' I offered, 'we can keep each other warm. All that glass, it gets cold in there at night.' The least I should do was keep an eye on her.

So we moved that day. Elizabeth didn't want to take much – clothes, the mattress and bedding. The conservatory had never been used to soak up the afternoon sun, entertain the neighbours, or cultivate cuttings. It was the office-cum-junk room. The only furniture was a tall steel filing cabinet, a cheap chipboard desk covered in peeling white plastic, the drawer handles long gone, and an old sofa, with plenty of spring left but no padding. There was always rubbish, of a sort, in the conservatory – bin bags of unwanted clothes for Oxfam, piles of magazines and papers and boxes of empty bottles for recycling that took months to leave the house.

So moving into the conservatory, odd though it was, actually meant a long overdue spring clean. Elizabeth was going to shove the bags of Oxfam clothes under the desk and the recycling bottles on top of the filing cabinet, but I thought it would be more cosy if we took them out. In fact I seized the moment and put them straight in the car to take into town later on. While I was clearing out, Elizabeth was reorganising the filing cabinet. She'd squeezed all the folders from the top drawers into the bottom and filled the empty drawers with her clothes. By the evening the conservatory looked, for the first time, homely.

Although it was cold in there at night Elizabeth never

complained, she just wore extra clothes. In fact mostly she didn't take her daytime clothes off. I still wore my pyjamas, out of habit I suppose. One night Elizabeth got fed up with my shivering and told me to put something warm on. 'If you can't keep still,' she warned, 'you can go back upstairs.' The next day I brought a blanket down but by bed time it had gone. I saw an edge sticking out behind the filing cabinet. 'Aren't you cold?' I asked later on when we were in bed. 'Not if I'm asleep,' she replied, in a common sense kind of way. I asked if she'd mind if I put a blanket on the bed. I didn't mention the one behind the filing cabinet. 'If you like,' she sighed, sounding indifferent. But then she must have minded because the next two blankets also ended up behind the filing cabinet. So I retrieved the three blankets and took them, my pyjamas and myself back up to the bedroom.

Elizabeth spent most of the daylight hours in the conservatory. The surface of the desk gradually disappeared and the clothes in the filing cabinet began to spill out. The duvet could barely be seen under more piles of clothes. She came out only to bring more things in. 'I've had enough of this,' she'd say, as she marched down the hall, her arms full of tea towels, or tablecloths, or jugs. Timmy and I would stand out of the way. 'How can you two live like this?' she'd ask, accusingly. We never said anything. We didn't know how we were living. Sometimes she'd want to move something too heavy or large, and then she'd call to one of us, point to an object and announce its destination – 'Timmy. Armchair. Conservatory.' That made sense – to make her new bedroom more cosy. Then one day it was 'Sam. Fridge. Conservatory.' I needed Timmy's help to move that one.

'We can't move it out of the kitchen,' muttered Timmy as we carried it down the hall. There wasn't much space for it in the conservatory, so we put it in front of the armchair. 'Dad, you've got to do something,' he pleaded, 'what good's the fridge in here?' He was right of course. Trudging down the hall whenever you wanted milk or margarine was going to get frustrating. We got used to it though – it was winter after all, so we could leave the essentials out on the kitchen window ledge.

After that, things started to get impractical. Elizabeth moved the chairs from the kitchen table into the hall and stacked them up, the legs entwined so it was impossible to get one down without the whole tower collapsing. Timmy mastered it though, and could stand on the stairs, lean over the banisters and unhook the top one. But then Elizabeth took all the plates and bowls off the dresser and stacked them inside the chair tower. They were awkward to fish out. Especially the ones that were stuck together with dried-up Weetabix or squashed strands of spaghetti.

The sink was full of dirty dishes too, including all the cutlery. In the mornings, I tried to wash up. I boiled the kettle for hot water instead of running the tap so Elizabeth wouldn't guess what I was up to. But it was hard to disguise the sound of knives and forks clattering against the steel sink. I tried singing, but could only ever remember nursery rhymes and after the first couple Elizabeth would shout at me to shut up. 'I can't concentrate,' she'd yell, or 'You're spoiling my peace of mind.' So I'd have to take each fork out one at a time and dry them individually. By the next day they were all dirty again. I imagined Elizabeth at night, sticking spoons into the jam, forks into the mustard and knives into the peanut butter.

The dresser, free from its usual collection of crockery, became home to an array of objects from all over the house. Some were recognisable. A collection of Seventies science fiction, some old books on trains that Elizabeth had inherited from her father, *How To Identify Sea Shells* and a Japanese phrase book. There were folders from the conservatory, of guarantees and instructions, mail order catalogues and reports from the children's school days. The middle shelves became increasingly full of unrecognisable objects. Things that had once been part of other things. Square plastic shapes with holes and slots, sheets of metal similarly perforated. Washers and bolts, wire and cable. Old torn clothes reduced to dusters then further transformed to abstract sculptural forms by hardened dirt. I didn't like to investigate these shelves in case I cut myself on a jagged edge.

I got frightened, though, when Elizabeth began to include my clothes in her rearranging plans. And she didn't just move them – I was used to that – it's a natural part of family life. No, this was different. She snatched clothes straight from the dirty laundry basket, took them apart and then stashed them somewhere else. A stripy wool jumper was partially unravelled and stuffed into the dresser alongside the unrecognisable plastic and metal components. A pair of not-so-old trainers, delaced and desoled, were thrown into one of the kitchen cupboards, breaking the handle off a mug in transit. I found pairs of my boxer shorts had been used to mop up spilt milk. And my jacket, its inside lining ripped out, was stuffed under the sink where fallen bottles of bleach continued its destruction.

I never saw Elizabeth doing it. I'd come down in the morning and find more of my clothes had been taken apart. My shirts became armless, my trousers lost their legs. One leg of a pair of cords had been used to wrap up the bones and skin of a roast chicken. Elizabeth was decimating my wardrobe and I realised I'd have to do something before I had no clothes left. So I packed one shirt, one pair of trousers, one pair of socks and one pair of boxer shorts into a plastic bag and squeezed it into the glove compartment of my car. I put a jumper under the driver's seat. I took to wearing a double set of everything too. It was winter anyway, so I didn't overheat.

Once I realised my car was a safe place – that Elizabeth didn't want to drive anywhere, or even spend any time outside – I relaxed. It was an old Volvo estate, so there was plenty of room to store my things. After the clothes were safely installed I began to assess what else needed protection. After all, Elizabeth might get bored of my clothes. I took CDs and books next. My top twenty of each. I tried to stick to ten, so the gaps on the shelves weren't too obvious, but I couldn't choose. I took some tools, basics for joinery. In a moment of nostalgia, I took a photo album – from when the boys were small. I took an old army blanket, a hand-me-down from my dad. Then I began spending time in the car. Sorting things out, disguising them. As Elizabeth never went outside I needn't have bothered, but this was my top twenty we were talking about. And I suppose I enjoyed the escape from the mess. A place I could keep tidy. I put a couple of cushions in and some days I brought a flask of coffee with me. I'd sit behind the wheel, not going anywhere, but listening to my music and turning the engine on now and again to keep the battery charged.

Timmy asked what I was doing. I think he might have

felt a bit abandoned in the house. He was still too young to drive then, so he'd come out to see if I was going anywhere. To catch a lift. I never was though and he didn't seem disappointed. He'd take his bike instead and cycle to the village shop. But he was always back soon and he'd always check on me on his way round to the back door. Sometimes with my music on I wouldn't hear him and he'd give me a fright tapping on the window. I'd wind the window down and he'd peer in. 'What you up to?' he'd ask, shuffling his feet and resting an elbow on the window. 'Oh nothing much,' I'd reply. It was hard to explain. He'd usually go inside then. Sometimes he left me a bar of chocolate from the shop. I enjoyed those days, sitting in the car. I felt like a rebellious teenager, sulking in my bedroom, playing loud music and annoying my parents. Only no one complained now. I was an adult and could do what I wanted after all.

When I came to spend whole mornings in the car though, things became a bit less comfortable. The windows were quickly covered in condensation and I couldn't open them without freezing. I'd run the engine for a while but the windows fogged up again as soon as I switched it off. So it made sense to go for a drive. I didn't tell anyone, which made it feel slightly illicit. Timmy asked me where I'd been the first few times and I'd say nonchalantly, 'Oh just taking the car for a spin.' He stopped asking after a while.

It was a dry February and the skies were often a pale fresh blue, with high clouds and a low sun. I'd drive onto the back roads on the other side of the valley, park up somewhere and look at our side of the valley from a different perspective. I was always surprised by the number of trees. I don't know why, since our house was surrounded by them. They stretched for miles in all directions, those trees. And most of them conifers, so the forest looked deep as well as wide. Then I got brave and drove over the top of the hills and looked down the other side. You could see the whole of the city to the north from there and all its satellite towns circling round. Sometimes I'd stay until the street lights came on, then they really did look like moons orbiting a mysterious, alluring planet.

It took a bit more courage to venture down from the hills. It's intoxicating, the view you get on high. I persuaded myself by saying it'd be good for me to see the valley hill tops from down there. Not that I didn't know the view from the city looking south — I'd driven along that road thousands of times going home. And of course I knew really, once I got there, I'd prefer to keep my eyes on the road ahead. I stopped a few times in the satellite towns to look for a high spot, but it was a half-hearted search. I was neither in one place or the other. That's suburbia for you, an unhappy compromise. So I drove on, taking the new motorway that sweeps downhill, across the river and into the city centre.

It was dark when I got there. Not late, but past rush hour so the roads were quiet. I found a twenty-four hour multi-storey carpark and slotted the car into a space on the top floor — a breezy, roofless, concrete plaza. Nothing but city to see from here. I took my bag, with my spare clothes, chose a CD and a book — my number ones you could say — and locked up the car. It was a smart new carpark, attached to a smart new shopping centre — restaurants on the top floor, boutiques on the others and glass lifts gliding up and down the facade, so you could see people outside and in. Making the whole world into a silent movie. From the carpark I could see the lights of individual shops, cars and street lamps below but from inside the lift, as it slid slowly towards the ground, I could no longer distinguish between them. All that glass — the lift, the buildings outside, car windscreens — made the reflections of lights bounce and contort. Once on the city street, out in the open, I could only see fifty yards in each direction and, at last, my view became reassuringly narrow.

Sonja Henrici

WAITING FOR NEPTUNE

I'm Salacia, the goddess of water, my mind seeps through
the streams, ponds, lakes and seas of this world.
In the middle of my ocean, Neptune towers, in full regalia,
his trident directs the water around him
like a conductor his orchestra.

On Sundays he'll cause no storm, he'll rest
on a stone instead. Tempted by the clear waters before him,
he'll decline to make them murky. I've tried
to swirl around him, to sweep him along with me,
added rain-drops to ripple the mirror pool he's cut for shaving.

But I've been kidding myself, I can't rush the currents
by weeping into them. I realise, they find their own pace.
I'm still learning about how lilies float and blossom,
how streams meander in serpentines, and seaweed grows,
how tides wax and wane, ebb and flood.

On Monday, I watch him step into work to walk upstream
until his heart's immersed. *Perhaps* he thinks *I should
rinse my hair?* and sinks with his head under.
I make myself invisible and send a school of fish on the watch –
he'll be surprised to meet a fidelity of happy flippers.

On Wednesday I get anxious for details. On Thursday
they report back to me: How he didn't trigger a single twister,
but how he got them into a whirl pool, free of charge,
and fed them every day with three course dinners of algae, flies
and breadcrumbs, while they taught him how to swim.

On Friday I emerge from the water for a change of scenery.
I amble over to his spot on the rock, watch myself gazing,
shivering from years in the rain, and wait there,
for the weather to change. It's still dry and hot.

On Saturday I dip my toes into the loch – at its warm and
    shallow end,
My fish squad drops by and nibbles at my feet.
I tell them, *I'll come back when I'm dry enough.*
– *Don't*, they whisper, *Wait here for Neptune, until tomorrow.*

John Heraghty

FALLING

Michael was falling. Falling backwards onto his bed. Falling onto his mattress. Falling into softness. And Gabriel was falling too. Falling on top of Michael. He could feel Gabriel's weight pressing against him, pinning him down. He could feel both their chests as they touched. Rising and falling. Rising and falling. Michael kissed Gabriel. The lips were soft and the breath was sweet. Michael liked the feeling.

Michael had been falling for years. He would trip on pavements, slip on polished floors and stumble down steps. Michael bumped into bus stops; fell off platforms and walked into glass doors. He didn't understand why it happened to him so often. When he was younger, if he tripped or stumbled he would be able to regain his balance and right himself. But now, once he felt the sensation of falling he would give in to the inevitable and prepare himself for the crash.

He put it down to age. He was getting older and was losing the ability to balance himself. Either that or he wasn't as flexible as he once was. Whatever the reason, Michael was crashing down all around the city. And he had the bumps to prove it. He was a regular visitor to the city's casualty departments. Sitting among the drunks, the football fans and the young children who had managed to get their finger stuck in some glass bottle or tin can, there was Michael who would be clutching his leg, holding on to his arm or nursing his head. A week never went by without a new bandage or dressing appearing on some part of his body.

You were holding your head the first time I saw you, Michael. You were standing outside a newspaper shop. Alone, on the street, with people rushing by. I didn't see what had happened but knew there must have been some sort of accident; had you walked into the door or tripped and banged your head of the glass window? I couldn't tell. But there you were, standing still, holding your head. All around you was movement. People going in and out of the shop, passing you by. No one stopped to ask if you were alright, if you needed help.

FALLING

> Some people, when they saw you, looked at the ground. Some deliberately changed their path to avoid you. As if you were trouble. Others didn't even notice you. Didn't stop to ask if you were alright. You looked embarrassed as if you wanted to apologise to everyone around you for putting them on the spot, for making them decide they were going to ignore you. I watched you regain a sense of where you were and then you started to walk away. Carefully now. Hesitant.

One day Michael was falling onto a road in town when Gabriel came along and caught him. Michael was waiting at a busy junction and was about to step down from the kerb onto the road when his attention was distracted by a brightly coloured chocolate wrapper floating on the wind. Michael liked the way the red and yellow wrapper flipped through the air, backwards and forwards, falling earthwards one moment and then, caught by a breeze, floating skywards again.

Michael followed the wrapper's path through the air and his attention drifted from the pavement. Like the chocolate wrapper he too was soon falling earthwards. He closed his eyes, prepared himself and thought about what part of his body would be injured this time. He was betting on his left knee. He remembered that when he stepped off the pavement it was his left leg that was leading, that was suspended in air, waiting to feel solid ground. So he reckoned, with his balance gone, this leg would buckle and his knee would take the impact.

So Michael was falling through air, thinking about his knee, about pain, about his trousers being ripped, about people looking at him, children laughing. On his way down he started to wonder how he could have so many thoughts in the short space of time it took to reach the ground. Then he felt himself being lifted up and soon he was standing upright on the pavement again.

– Okay? Are you okay? A voice asked.
– Yes. I'm fine. I think so, Michael replied.

Two hands were on his shoulders, holding him up. Michael turned round and saw a man smiling at him. The man let go of his shoulders.

– You have to watch these pavements, the man said, they're treacherous.
– I know, Michael said, I'm always falling.

– I'm Gabriel, Hello.
– Michael. I'm Michael.
Michael, after I saw you in the street that first time and you walked off, I followed. I followed you for days after that. I walked behind you, watching you look at the people, at the buildings. Your head going from side to side, taking everything in. As I watched you I started to see what you saw. The colours and the shapes and the people. I looked at things too but I didn't see what you saw. I didn't see colours. I only saw black and white and grey. Everything was in straight lines for me. You saw shapes and patterns everywhere. I followed you around the city; watching you for a long time. Falling, getting back up. Falling again and getting back up again. Starting over. Then, one day, I was really close. I was right behind you. At your shoulder. You didn't know I was there. And then you started to crumple, to go down in slow motion. I reached out for you.

They stood in the middle of the street and shook hands. Michael's hand disappeared into Gabriel's. Gabriel covered it over and Michael could feel it warm and strong. He wanted his hand to stay in Gabriel's for a long time.

When Michael began to fall with some regularity it started to worry his family. Getting old, head in the clouds he would say in order to reassure them. He started to worry himself when it happened more frequently and he couldn't do anything about it. He saw his doctor, told him his concerns and had a series of tests done. Nothing was found. The doctors told him to carry on as normal but to be more careful, to look where he was going. Look at the roads, step round the potholes and avoid the high pavements they said. This worked and while he kept his mind on his surroundings he never fell. His bruises and cuts soon mended but the concentration he needed was exhausting. When he came home in the evening he would flop down in the chair, tired out from concentrating on the streets all day.

He didn't want to be staring at the ground all day every day. Michael enjoyed his walks too much and liked being able to look about him. He enjoyed looking at the way the sky changed as the day passed. He liked looking into shop windows when there was a new display. He gained a deep pleasure when a new building was being erected on old waste ground and watched in wonder as the foundations were put in, scaffolding went up, brick walls appeared and then after months, sometimes the best part of a year, piece by piece, the scaffolding came back down again, and something solid and substantial was revealed. Something new. Something just created.

So Michael got fed up poring over the potholes, stanks, kerbs and railings that were all over the city. Being out in the open air, watching the city, day in day out was something he wasn't about to give up. So Michael thought he would take his chances. Soon he was falling all over again. That's when Gabriel turned up.

When Michael eventually let go of Gabriel's hand he said thanks once more and continued on his journey. But over the next few days as Michael was making his way around the streets, concentrating on not falling but always failing, Gabriel would appear at his shoulder and catch him. He would lift him back up again.

– Thanks again, Michael would say.

– No problem. I saw you from across the road, Gabriel would answer. Lucky I was in the area.

Soon Michael stopped worrying about falling; he knew that Gabriel would be there to catch him. He started to look forward to the sensation of weightlessness; the few moments he would have falling through air. But now instead of preparing himself for the worst, instead of breaking out in a cold sweat, Michael would wait for the strong hands to appear on his shoulder. He would think about the grip, light at first and then firm and solid as Gabriel took hold of him and lifted him back onto his feet.

Now when he left the house in the morning he calculated when his first fall would occur, when he would see Gabriel again. Would it be at the traffic lights, or the roundabout or near the bus stop? The bus stop was particularly treacherous. There was a shop nearby that sold wallpaper and Michael liked looking at the swirling patterns. Once his eye caught the bright colours and shapes of the wallpaper it would only be a matter of seconds before he would be walking into the metal poles that supported the bus shelter. But not any more. He could look at the wallpaper in total confidence and also be sure that Gabriel would put himself between him and the cold metal supports.

– You again, Michael would say, in a surprised tone, knowing all the time that Gabriel would appear.
– Me again, yes, Gabriel would say apologetically. You probably think I am following you, don't you.
– No. Not at all. I'm just glad you're around.
– As long as you're not bothered.
– I'm not bothered, Michael said.

He definitely wasn't bothered. He wasn't bothered when Gabriel asked him to go for a coffee. He wasn't bothered when Gabriel took him back to his flat. Michael wasn't bothered when Gabriel started to kiss him. Gabriel's kisses were soft on Michael's cheek. Soft on his neck, on his forehead, on his arms. Soft all over his body. His kisses were gentle and warm. Michael felt the warmth of Gabriel's lips. Lips trembling and pulsing with blood and life. Putting his life on Michael's body. Sharing himself with him. Michael never knew anything like it before.

When they were together Gabriel didn't say much. He listened. He listened to Michael talking. Michael told him all about his problems on the city streets, about how his family were worried about him. And he told Gabriel that sometimes he felt scared too, that maybe there was something wrong with him, something horrible, something lying dormant in him that no one could find but would come to the surface any day now and change his life forever.

Gabriel put his hand on top of Michael's and he stopped talking. Michael looked at the hand. The skin was white and clear, the fingers long and slender. The nails were perfectly cut. Michael felt calm when Gabriel put his hand on top of his. Gabriel took his hand away.

– There's nothing wrong with you, he said.

Michael didn't say anything. He looked at Gabriel and believed him.

You told me your name was Michael and shook my hand. Your hand in mine was small. I didn't want to let go. You didn't want to let go. I knew instantly that I would stay with you. Guard you. Look after you. From that day on. I didn't want to be on the outside any longer. Watching but never belonging. I didn't want to be an observer any more. Looking down on people all the time. Distant, cold and detached. Watching people make mistakes and then covering them up. Pretending they didn't happen. Making sure no one else saw.

Everyone saw your mistakes, Michael. You were on the street. Out in the open. There was no hiding place. Everyone saw you falling. Saw you get it wrong. I saw you too. Saw you pick yourself up and go on. Now I go on too.

Michael's falling again. Falling into Gabriel's arms. Gabriel opens his arms wide and embraces him. Welcomes him in. He wraps his arms around Michael and holds him close. Michael loves to fall now. There is no fear. There is no hard tarmac. No pain. No watching eyes. No children laughing. No humiliation. There is no fear, only certainty. Only Gabriel. Catching him, picking him up. Putting him gently back on his feet.

Duncan Jones

URBAN MYTHS
Folk Tales of the Glaswegians, translated from the demotic by Joseph H. Presswell, FRS

Billy and Big Man
Billy was always marching up and down the streets of the city. Whum, whum, whum, went his big round drum. Eee-whee-eee, went his little tin flute, and the bright orange sash he always wore swung from side to side.

The other people in the city would complain, 'Why are you always marching up and down the streets of the city, Billy? Why do you have to make so much noise? Give us peace!' But Billy didn't listen to them. He was proud of his big round drum, and his little tin flute, and the noises they made. He was proud, too, that everyone paid so much attention to him. He would stop at all the junctions, and bang on his drum until the air throbbed, so that nobody would miss him going past: whum, WHUM, whum, whum!

Billy worked his way up and down all the streets, making sure that he went through every part of the city. But one day he turned a corner and found himself in Big Man's neighbourhood. 'Well,' he thought to himself, 'now's my chance to let Big Man see what a fine fellow I am!' And he went WHUM, WHUM, WHUM, and EEE-WHEE-EEE, and he stamped his feet at the crossroads.

Then what happened? Listen: Big Man had had a heavy night, and was sleeping soundly. Then the whumming of the drum made his windows rattle, and the eeeing of the flute went through his ears like two points of ice. He shot out of bed, and ran to the window. 'What is all that banging and shrieking?' he roared. 'Can't a man get a bit of sleep around here?'

Big Man flung back the curtains, and the early morning light made his eyes stream. All he saw was a big orange shape at the crossroads, but he could tell that was where the noise was coming from. He pulled on his boots, picked up his chib, and ran downstairs onto the street.

Billy saw him coming. 'Good morning, Big Man!' he shouted over the noise of his drum. 'See what a fine fellow I

am! Nobody can ignore me. Even you want to come out and get a proper look at me!'
'Stop making that terrible noise!' Big Man yelled. 'Give us peace!' But Billy wouldn't stop. He puffed out his chest until his orange sash seemed to cover his whole body. 'Give us peace!' shouted Big Man again. 'You're inconveniencing everybody. Stop being so selfish.'
'I don't care,' replied Billy. 'Why should I do anything for anyone else?'
'I'll show you why,' roared Big Man, and he slashed at Billy with his chib. Billy cried out, and tried to run away: but he found he couldn't move. He tried to throw away his big round drum and his little tin flute, but they were stuck fast to him. He started to swell up and up and out and out, and got bigger and bigger and squarer and squarer until he was a great big box, twice as tall as he was wide and twice as long as he was tall. He tried to call for help, but the only sounds he could make were whum, whum, whum, and eee-whee-eee.
'Now,' said Big Man, 'you like to travel up and down all the streets of the city, do you?' And he tore big black pieces of rubber from off his boots, and rolled them into tyres. He stuck them all around the four corners of the great big box that Billy had become. Then he took his chib and cut windows all around the sides, one row above the other. 'Well, from now on that's what you shall do. And to make up for all the trouble you've caused, you will have to carry all the people of the city about with you.'
From that time on Billy became a Number 57 bus, and had to travel all around the city, up and down all the streets, carrying the people wherever they wanted to go. If you look closely at his paintwork you can see his orange sash underneath, and you can still hear him at the junctions, going whum, whum, whum on his big round drum. Sometimes as he goes along the road you can hear him blowing his flute, eee-whee-eee, too. But he does it quietly, in case Big Man has had another heavy night.

Pigeon's Voice
Back before you were born, Pigeon was considered to be the most attractive man in the city. All the women said so; partly because he dressed so well, in such fine clothes. Most

of all, though, it was because of his beautiful voice. When he spoke, his words were dark and soft as Guinness, but when he sang – oh, when he sang, the girls would blush and the women would smile. They all loved him, and didn't he just know it?

A lot of men admired him; a lot of men were jealous of him, too. And no-one was more jealous of Pigeon than Seagull. Seagull didn't have an easy time with women. He looked good, from a distance, white and clean against the sky; but up close, they said, he had a big nose. Big, flat feet, too, that smelled of fish. He always laughed at his own rotten jokes, and what a laugh! It was like having ice-cubes poured into your ears, they said. Needless to say, he couldn't sing to save himself.

And this is really what made Seagull so jealous. Mostly he was just nervous around women. Everything he wanted to say would sound so stupid inside his own head that he would panic, rattle off some terrible patter instead and then laugh to try to drown it out. But, he noticed, nothing sounded stupid when you sang it. He listened to Pigeon's lyrics and saw that, without the music of that voice behind them, they were just sentimental mush. 'Baby-maybe,' he would mutter to himself, 'Kissin'-missin'. Lovin'-Govan!' he would snort, and his jealousy grew and grew.

Eventually he could stand it no more. He began to spy on Pigeon, to see if he could find some way to bring him down. One day, at a bus stop, he got an idea. Pigeon came strolling past, arm in arm with a pretty girl. She was offering him a cigarette. 'Not for me, baby,' Pigeon said, before turning his head and murmuring in her ear, 'Bad for the *voice.*' They laughed, and cuddled in closer, and walked on.

The next day, Seagull went to see Pigeon at his flat. 'What can I do for you?' asked Pigeon, standing at his front door. 'Hey, wait, haven't I seen you around somewhere?'

'Possibly,' said Seagull. 'I've taken a bit of an interest in you. I'm in the music industry, and I think you have real potential.'

'Oh, I've got potential, man,' said Pigeon, smugly.

'Well, I can help you turn that potential into something big. Singing in pubs and on the street isn't good enough for that voice of yours. I could make you a star!' And that's just what he did.

Seagull started small, and got Pigeon a few paid gigs on the outskirts of the city. Then the venues got a little bigger; local halls and community centres, then concert halls and finally a tour. 'Your profile's going up, Pigeon!' Seagull would say. 'There's big things coming your way!'

Pigeon worked hard. He'd always been really laid-back, but Seagull had convinced him that success was just around the corner. It looked that way, too; there was money coming in, although Pigeon never seemed to have any time to spend it. 'I'll take care of the bills, Pigeon,' Seagull would say. 'I've got a head for figures. You just work that golden voice.'

Pigeon had begun to attract a real following. They liked his old songs, but Seagull convinced him to write new ones, too. 'I know it's hard work,' he would say, sympathetically, 'but that's why it's called an industry. It'll be worth it, though, when your first album comes out. There's a couple of labels who are *definitely* interested in you!' Pigeon, dreaming of his coming fame and fortune, would work long into the night writing new material. Seagull moved into Pigeon's flat, 'To help you keep your focus,' he said.

All the hard work took its toll, though. Pigeon got more and more exhausted, and with sitting up late eating snacks and junk food he began to put on weight. It was Seagull who convinced him to start smoking.

'But what about my voice?' Pigeon cried.

'Hey, don't worry. How can a few cigarettes hurt something as wonderful as the *voice*? If anything, some smoke will just add a sexy little edge. You don't have to inhale or anything. Mostly it's just about the image. And they'll help you concentrate, and keep you looking good.'

So Pigeon started smoking. At first it was just one or two, and mostly he'd just wave them around. But soon enough he was smoking ten, then twenty, then forty and sixty a day. Seagull would see Pigeon sitting at all hours in front of his piano, chaining his way through whole packs as he scribbled down songs, his fine clothes all grey-dusted with ash. When Seagull heard him leave the flat in the black hours before the dawn to walk a long mile through the rain to the all-night garage, he turned over in bed and smiled a secret smile at the dark bedroom wall.

One morning, as Pigeon stood by the sink waiting for the kettle to boil, he felt a tickle in his throat. 'Hrum,' he said. 'Hur-hur-hur-hrum.' He coughed. He coughed again. He coughed and coughed and coughed until ping! he coughed his voice right up. It shot out of his mouth, a beautiful little golden ring, hit the edge of the sink and bounced out of the window. It spun through the cold morning air, fell into the gutter and rolled plop down a drain. Some say it rolled all the way to the sea, where a big fish swallowed it right up just like it shows on the coat of arms.

Pigeon was horrified. He tried to call for help, but all that came out was a throaty 'hroo!' He rushed through to Seagull's room. 'Hroo! Hroo!' he cried, tears streaming down his face. But Seagull was gone, along with all the money.

Pigeon has never sung again since that day. He still clears his throat, over and over, and does his best to attract the girls with it. Even with all that's happened to him, he's never been able to give up cigarettes. He spends most of his days now scratching in the gutter; people say he's searching for his voice, but really he's just looking for doups. When he finds one he lights it up, blowing the smoke out of his nostrils in two little puffs straight up into the air. And Seagull wheels over his head, laughing and laughing and laughing.

Beth Junor

ASUNDER

Praise the particularity of moments
for the timing of waves, for that moment
I looked up, saw you drawing the bamboo blinds
for the day, and for just that moment you looked down,
waved. Somewhere a child jumped, meeting the sea.
That afternoon, I removed the Summer's

dead growth from my plants, prepared for Winter
and planted for Spring. All that day we left each other,
my ring on your hand now, as if a betrothal had taken place,
my thumb kept meeting my ring finger – a talismanic habit.
I was continually surprised, not so much by absence
as by this new presence, the everything of you.

Praise the synchronicity of moon, tide and lovers'
breath, rising and falling in the dark, in black and white
rooms filled with objects that will outlast love. Praise this stillness
lasting before colour and movement arrive and we interrupt
the order of things. The kettle is moved to the stove,
tealeaves continue journeying thousands of miles.

Now the moon is full, whiter and brighter
than the Haymarket clock beneath her. Time
celestial and earthly. Between, the silence that makes me
who I am. We're apart and the world will continue
as she is, strapping destruction to her midriff,
moving inexorably towards fragmentation.

WINTER SOLSTICE

Here it's just dark and cold.

In the French market
    the generator
    keeps going
                    off
    and I can't see
the glaze of the pottery
from Morocco, nor
        recapture the warmth
of that night in Paris
    when another generation
    of street traders worked.

At my own work's Christmas
    lunch, my colleague who drops
        drugged tears into her eyes
        every three hours
           tells me

there's much more light out there

than we allow ourselves
to see.   The radio

    announces a webcam's
        in place at Maes Howe
    for the Solstice. She's right,

I don't dare to watch online

the sun striking the back
        of the chamber.

Kirsten Kearney

PSALM 23

Goodness and love run to catch up
I have left them counting their toes
At the start of the mountain path.

The oil pools in the frying pan
I take and eat, and safely
Extinguish the flame.

My knees are my table
Set with humble fare, my enemies
I could count on one hand.

The rod and staff are cheerleaders' tools
The sheep had their legs broken
They hung round the shepherd's neck.

Psalm 23 has oiled the coils of death
It is too insistent. It props open
The swinging door of hope.

The waves and breakers are unquiet
We move for the safe pasture
Climb for the higher ground.

Down in the muck-heap of the world
We have been scattered.
But we shall begin to want.

Lis Lee

BUSH FIRE

In the canopy
flame bangles skin,
leaves and eyes weep smoke,
pelts singe, wood arcs.

Airborne waters spill and boil,
hoses fire a hot fog.
Dribbles, seeking soil,
ring limb and bark crease.

It was safe inside flesh,
behind closed eyes. Tails hooked
sleeping branches. Now,
molten x-rays hang.

Joanna Lilley

THIEF

He likes the scrape of stone on skin as he climbs cold granite. Enjoys the pull of muscle and tendon after seated hours of driving. Too heavy, he snaps a birch branch but, looking up, no shallow wingbeats return deep-chested parents to their ledge; their circlings and stoops are not for him. In the hand, one egg looks too small. To have driven so far, climbed so high. It's easy to reach for the other three. *Falco peregrinus* will be back next year to breed again; all he will cause is brief confusion. The drive home is quick and slow as anticipation and congratulation dance. At home, the final work is soon done. The needle slides in, holing shell and membrane – both ends – to release a smell of egg. Blowing the gluey dribbling contents out and flushing them down a toilet. Arranging the empty cases on velvet beside last year's batch; a heavier, riper crop when it had not been as easy to expel the lives inside, when he had poured acid into a larger needle hole to dissolve the downy contents. A flesh smell then, not egg.

DISAPPOINTMENT

Layers of fat, like tree-trunk rings, protect her from each year of disappointment. The hopes, solidified, adhere to her middle, squeezed as she bends to tie up another bin-liner of clothes that no longer fit. She lifts the bag into her car at night and sets it down outside the locked doors of the Barnardo's shop at dawn. Last time, it was Help the Aged; she alternates charities according to which flowers first: regret or fear. The fruits of disappointment, she knows, cannot ripen into failure if they are watered with hope. She draws a picture of a watering-can on a post-it and sticks it on the fridge.

EMIGRANT

When she told her family she was going to emigrate, she forgot she was related to her country too. Each day, as she prepared to go, she remembered the guilt of leaving parents too ill to travel across an ocean and a precambrian shield of rock to her new home. Each day, she remembered the guilt of leaving a sister and nieces who could not afford the flight. And she remembered – less often and with less guilt – that, if she was careless enough, she might forget to give some of her friends her new address. It was on a farewell tour of her country's highest peaks that, balanced on Carn Mor Dearg ridge, she realised the granite she was clinging to didn't care if she was there or not, and yet she wished it did.

Stuart Robert Macdonald

JOCK STEINBECK ON RUE OSGOODE, OTTAWA

End of August, mid-morning

After kicking a ball about with boys who said they were
   from Rideau
I stretched out on the rough grass beside e a s y – g o i n g
   traffic
and sprinkled blue seeds of sky over my washed out eyes

late morning in the imago orchard
my mind picked its 10000th apple...
....

so I got down from my cider-rusted ladder
to celebrate.

All of us went to Mac's to buy clinky bags of party food

we invited Rhuari from the laundrette,
his tales are word tunes of light escaping from a
   kaleidoscope prison.

I knew I was someway behind Gillis from Cape Breton
his applehappy mind had picked 87028 and counting
aon, dha, tri, ceithir, coig, sia... his way back to Ingonish

so the firewater started to flow,
blackbirds, sparrows, bees danced
to our mouth music
and the ghostwritten echo of piped dreams.

Deflected by concrete,
pinball breezes scattered leaves of air
in and around us
while we sat roaming the memories
of thousands of displaced men

and under the tangerine gaze of the heat,
as someone wrote much later in a story called
Technicolor Heritage of Lewisian Gneiss,
we looked like plastic cartoons
melting our lives away, away
melting our lives away.

ACETO BALSAMICO DI MODENA

Nice on chips or
a hot Malone's bridie

stimulates the senses
on a lard fried egg

so with the empty bottle
out goes the last dregs

of your cool refinement
I hoped to suffuse.

All that remains is
the bruises of losing

my taste buds, numb
to finer things in life

and I know it's sour grapes
but at least in the mornings

I didn't take sugar
on my hot porridge oats.

Morag McDowell

PONDLIFE

Gail is in the bath practising survival. She floats quietly with only the slightest touch of her fingertips on the bottom, then pushes her head down and back until the tepid water runs into her ears, creeps over her forehead, rushes into her nostrils. It feels invasively cold but she knows she must get used to it. She lets her body arch like a crab, and counts 31, 32, 33 seconds. She imagines sweeping down backwards to the darkness of a river bed, doing a somersault then coming up, her body straight as a bullet, taut and slim enough to fit through the smallest window.

It is essential to stay calm as panic will only use up precious oxygen.

Her chest feels like an over-inflated balloon. Earlier than usual, the blood starts to pound through her head, then she realises that mother is hammering on the door.
 'Get out of the fucking bathroom, Birthday Girl!'
 She stands up, taking a deep sucking breath and wraps a towel around her body, listening. When the footsteps have receded downstairs, she opens the door. The phone is lying on the hallway carpet at her feet.
 'Hello?'
 'Hiya Princess! Many happy returns!'
 'Hi Dad.'
 'How's my girl, then? Fourteen years old, I can't believe it.'
 He's on his mobile and it sounds like there's a hurricane blowing. She can hear muttering downstairs, where is it, where is it, then the sound of a glass smashing and cursing. He's saying something about her present.
 'What?'
 'I said, you'll get it at the weekend, okay?'
 'Dad, can I ask you something?'
 'Sure...' His words are torn apart by static. She imagines him being picked up, swirled around and blown far into the distance, the phone still clamped to his ear.
 'Dad?'

There is a blast of fresh air as, downstairs, the front door opens, car keys jangle, mother shouts, 'Two minutes!'
The line's dead. Gail puts the phone down, takes a deep breath, walks past mother's bedroom door and starts counting. It's not just because of the dreams that she does it. The air is overloaded. There's the central heating, turned on full even though it's summer, there are the mangy red velvet curtains in the living-room, hanging from their poles like giant collapsed lungs, emitting faint puffs of cigarette smoke and spilled booze and there are the various aromas of mother's perfumes and essential oils — Eternity and *appassionata* left open to evaporate on the dressing-table, Virginian Cedarwood and cold-pressed Bergamot spilled and forgotten, bleaching the wood of the medicine cabinet shelves. Worst of all though, is the cupboard in the small upstairs hallway, which Gail creeps past now. Inside is a swamp of bursting carrier bags and crumbling shoe-boxes filled with damp and mildewed photographs. She looked at them once and saw a slim girl with short black hair and a baby in her arms. She saw her father standing in the front garden of an old Victorian house, smiling manically, one hand pushing back an unlikely mop of thick brown hair. Behind the boxes are bin bags full of old clothes, drainpipe jeans, size ten, a red satin ballgown, size eight. Gail's been told the girl is mother, the clothes are mother's and the baby is herself just after she was born, but it's all musty old lies to her. The only things to be trusted are the bottles at the very back which are usually empty but still redolent of bitter-sweet gin or syrupy Christmas liqueur. They are cleaned away occasionally, then others magically reappear, in the cupboard and elsewhere, sparkling darkly from unexpected corners like fairy mushrooms. She makes a run for it and crashes into her bedroom, wishing she could get a door with an airlock fitted.

Close your eyes, take deep steady breaths and imagine your heartbeat beginning to slow down.

In the kitchen there is a card waiting. It has a picture of a mermaid on it and, in shiny pink letters, 'To a Dear Daughter from your Loving Mum'. It isn't signed but there's money inside. She puts it in her skirt pocket, eats a bowl of cornflakes, drinks a can of Coke. Through the slats of the blind, she sees mother putting her briefcase and laptop into the car, a blue Fiat Punto supplied by the school book company for whom she now works as a sales manager. She used to be a school teacher, until one night when Gail was twelve, she'd come home and said, 'I've resigned!' then pulled Gail close till her face was only inches away and whispered, 'Never apologise, never explain.'

Gail's nostrils had flooded with the smell of cough mixture and smoked haddock. She'd recognised the last of the malt whisky her father had left behind, held her breath discreetly and counted to 30 before mother released her.

'I'm going! Now!'

Gail runs, grabbing her schoolbag and jacket. By the time she closes the front door, mother is in the driver's seat, revving the engine. She's wearing her black trouser suit and the high-heeled pointy-toed boots that make it difficult for her to brake properly. Her make-up is careful, flawless. For a moment Gail thinks of the smiling face locked in the hallway cupboard, then mother leans over into a shaft of 8am sunlight. The face bloats, dark lividly coloured shadows appear, floating underneath the surface of Max Factor Time Delay Translucence and it's as though the photograph girl's been left at the bottom of the river for a few days.

'Stop flapping your mouth like a guppy and get in the car.'

Gail opens the passenger door obediently, takes a deep breath and gets in. Mother clenches her teeth and pulls out violently into the oncoming traffic.

'Don't forget we're going out tonight. To celebrate.'

'Is Marina coming?'

'We're meeting her at the restaurant.'

Gail fastens her seat belt, wondering hopefully if her elder sister's presence will lighten the mood, then smiles, suddenly remembering she has double biology that morning. Dissecting frogs. She likes it when she has school on her birthday.

Once the car has settled on the bottom, open the windows an inch or so and let it fill with water so that the pressure inside is equal to the pressure outside.

She gets home first that afternoon, lets herself in then takes the stairs two at a time, not breathing until she has reached her room and closed the door behind her. The dark green curtains are still drawn. She crosses to her dressing-table where hairbrushes and make-up have been swept away to make room for a large illuminated fish-tank. She opens the lid and sprinkles food on the water. Swordtails and Lemon Tetras quiver to the surface, light from the tank undulates gently around the walls. She switches on a lamp, sits down at a small desk and writes a report on her frog dissection, drawing the heart and entrails in microscopic detail, knowing she will get an A, she always does. As she finishes, the front door slams. She hears the clacking of heels on the wooden stairs, the creak of a door opening, then the sound of a match being struck and a long, slow exhalation of breath. Mother officially stopped smoking the day after Gail informed her, inaccurately, that her father was planning to run the London Marathon. Gail puts her pen down and imagines the white smoke curling round inside mother's ribcage, turning the delicate pink capillaries into crispy fried duck. There are so many ways to die, she thinks, takes a deep breath and starts to count. Stocking-soled feet pad softly past her door and down the stairs then from the kitchen she hears the chink of ice in a glass.

She takes out of her wardrobe a party dress that was bought for her last Christmas and tries it on. It is shorter than before and uncomfortably tight across the chest. She takes it off and looks in the mirror behind the fish tank. Reflections of air bubbles from the filter stream across her bare shoulders and breasts. 32, 33, 34. Her ears are ringing. She closes her eyes and sees herself naked and beautiful, like a siren singing from a rock, then in a white coat as a brilliant scientist or a surgeon who makes last-minute life-saving incisions like the one that was made in mother's belly before Gail was hauled out, screaming and bloody, irritatingly alive. A car horn blares. Gail blinks, pulls the dress back on and goes into the hallway to see mother standing at the bottom of the stairs, examining her face in a compact mirror,

stretching her lip-sticked mouth over her teeth in an unnaturally wide smile. Gail says,
'You look nice.'
Mother pulls at the buttons of the green silk blouse she's wearing.
'The taxi's here.'

As the car fills with water, start to take slow deep breaths. Before it fills completely, take one last deep breath, let yourself go under the surface, and locate the door handle.

Gail's stomach starts to churn when they stop at Pagganinni's.
'I thought we were going to Pizza Hut.'
'Let your father take you to Pizza Hut. It's more his style. Where the hell is she? What did he get you anyway?'
'He hasn't had time to get anything yet, he's been so busy training – for his run, you know? He says I can pick what I like on Saturday.'
Mother looks impatiently up and down the street for Gail's older sister, muttering,
'What a prick!' then waves, smiling brightly. Gail sees Marina walking languidly towards them. Three months of student life have changed her. She no longer sports the dark brown mass of American cheerleader curls, which Gail has envied for years. Her hair is short and spiky. She looks smug but her arms feel thin as she gives Gail a hug,
'Alright frog face? Wow, get a new bra.' She leans close and whispers in her ear,
'I'll buy you a present when I get my loan. How is she?'
Marina has never whispered anything to her in front of mother. Before Gail can recover from the shock and reply, her sister is pulled away,
'Darling, it's been so long since we've seen you, and how is university?'
Mother takes Marina by the arm and leaves Gail to walk behind. Gail sees through the windows of the restaurant that the manager has noticed them and is rushing to open the door. Mother is saying to Marina,
'I knew it was worth questioning your grades. There's a world of difference between university and the local college. Hairdressers, beauty therapists and motor mechanics, that's what you'd have got there. Pond life, darling, pond life.'

Her voice is too loud. The manager is smiling like a demented chat show host, saying, 'What a surprise, Mrs Donaldson!' He takes mother's coat, shows them to a table near the window, the one mother likes. Gail wishes they were at the back wall, where there is a mural of a Roman villa at the side of a lake which merges at the bottom into blue floor tiles. A bottle of wine is delivered to their table without their having to ask. Their order is taken quickly and within five minutes of sitting down they are on the main course although it is busy and other tables are still waiting to be served. Gail looks around defensively while her mother talks through her linguini al porcini. People walking past outside look in with vague curiosity as she waves her fork about to illustrate a point. There is a globule of cheese sauce on the bosom of her blouse. It looks like a small white wart.

The door of the car should now open easily.

Gail takes a deep breath, closes her eyes and she's in the dream. She and Marina are sitting in the back of a car. Sometimes her father is in the passenger seat, sometimes not, but mother is always driving, too fast, towards the edge of a wooden jetty. She's talking loudly but Gail can't hear what she's saying because she's too worried that mother's looking at them and not seeing where the car's heading. Gail screams at her to turn around but it's too late and they are flying through the air in freefall towards the surface of the water. It ripples softly, like a silk sheet, like Marina's hair, but Gail knows the whooshing muffled thump the car will make as it hits. She opens her eyes. A second bottle of wine has been delivered to their table. Her mother is still talking, but Gail can't hear. It's as though she's put seashells to her ear, like she did when she was small. The waves are booming in then falling back, hissing on the sand. The restaurant manager is hovering, nearby. Marina is smiling, but her eyes are sliding about from the windows to the front door to the fire exit.

'Gail, what is wrong with you?'

Gail blinks. Mother's face is close enough for her to see lipstick starting to bleed into the tiny cracks around her mouth. She is giving Gail the same puzzled scowl that she gives the video recorder when she hasn't programmed it

properly. She sighs theatrically, turns to Marina to say something but suddenly puts her hand up to her lips which are half open and instead of words there comes an enormous growling belch. Suddenly Gail can hear everything with amazing clarity – ice cubes rattling in glasses, a hiss of steam from the kitchens, someone in the far corner giggling. Marina stands up,
'I'm going.'
She lifts her jacket from the chair and leaves.
Mother hasn't moved or spoken. Her hand is still halfway to her mouth. Her eyes are wide, the pupils dark and dilated. She could be having a stroke, Gail thinks calmly, she could be dead, sitting in a car filled with water. 45, 46, 47, Gail exhales gently and picks up the menu, wondering if she should ask for Tiramisu.
They get a taxi home. Gail pays the driver while mother finds her keys and opens the front door. The phone is ringing. Gail lifts the handset as mother slowly climbs the stairs.
'Hiya Princess, can you hear me now?'
'Hi Dad.'
'Had a good birthday?'
'We went to Pagannini's. Marina came. Dad? You know that book you left?'
'What book?'
'The one about survival.'
'I don't think it's one of mine.'
'There's a chapter in it about what to do if you're in a car and it crashes into water. You have to wait till the car settles on the bottom, then open the door and swim out.'
'It's not my book.'
'You'd have to hold your breath for a long time, wouldn't you, and what if you couldn't get the door open. What if the electrics go and it gets stuck?'
'Look, we'll talk about it on Saturday. 12.30? Usual place?'
She replaces the handset, goes into the kitchen and takes from a cupboard a bottle of whisky. She puts the kettle on, pours the whisky into a mug until it is half full then adds three teaspoons of sugar. When the kettle is boiled she fills the mug, gives it forty seconds in the microwave then carries it carefully up the stairs.

Do not panic. You need only to push off, kick gently and you will float to the surface. Remember your body is 90% water. You are light and buoyant. You are at home in this element and if you stay calm it will not defeat you. It may help to remove your shoes.

She knocks and waits. Where there's no reply, she takes a deep breath and opens the door. The bedside lamp is on, its beam illuminating the green blouse in ripples on the floor, the blue silk sheets sliding off the bed, leaving mother's breasts and stomach exposed. They are pale and still, an arrangement of smooth bleached rocks or dunes at the bottom of an ocean trench. Gail thinks at first that she's sleeping, but then mother moves and suddenly sits up, panicky fingers reaching for the sheet, pulling it around her. Her hair is sticking out in clumps, straying into the air like sea grass. Her mascara is running in black rivulets down her cheeks. She looks at Gail, who holds the mug out towards her.

'What's in it, Paraquat?'

Gail shakes her head, counting 35, 36, 37. Mother takes the mug, brings it slowly towards her lips. The liquid is still almost boiling, Gail can feel her eyes watering in the hot alcohol-laden steam. She wants to say, 'Never apologise, never explain,' but she's at 48 seconds and going for the minute.

James McGonigal

THE CAMPHILL WREN

For days I've come back to the wren
that takes flight from my doorstep
or fossicks in honeysuckle for spiders.
Tonight it escapes me again
to merge with dead leaves in the hedgefoot.

'Ah,' my ornithological Irish friend
concurs, expert in fauna and verses,
'The wren is not an easy bird to start
a poem on.' Its wing beats
sweep the doorstep empty as a heart.

As I stepped out one summer morning
with thoughts of our grandchild awake in France,
a spool unravelled just at the height
of this hand where she fed before – wrens
part from honeysuckle as carelessly as that,

each having taken its fill and turned
small as a leaf in the dry hedgefoot.
Once-in-a-decade sightings
made me think that the wren was declining –
but no, Gerry says: only for years I've had my eye
                                      on other things.

PREPARATIONS FOR EASTER

She was sheltering in the church porch
from a sharp wind and the gossip
and he was there in its half-dark too,
taking a break from his mowing.
Holy Week notices, posters for pilgrimages,
a diocesan letter twitched in the draught
as we opened the outer door and stepped inside.

She had a beautiful head, and was taller than he was
and heavier too, I'd say, her jeans were tight
across backside and thighs. And she was hanging
on his every word, and hanging on his every silence.
Magdalene mistook her risen Christ for a gardener,
but there was no mistaking the reek of grass and petrol
off this one, overpowering the perfume from her blouse.

In church, all of the statues were hooded in purple
for Good Friday. Out in the porch, her eyes were starry
for the wee gardener with the crush
of the first mown grass of April on his boots.

Which man here among us would not turn
from his own devotions at the thought of hers?

THE HALF-AWAKE SOUL

The years of my soul have passed
like the warmth of a bed
under sheets of moonlight or rain.
The length of my soul has turned over
from one side to the other.

The best months were spent in silence,
they were passing over into silence.
I'll say no more about that
breath silvering life's mirror,
nor tell who was glimpsed there.

I remember whole weeks passed at ease
stretched out on the new grass in May,
or awake as the sea is now,
turning waves to a lather of light
in the channels of night.

The best days all had their moments
caught in birdsong or birdflight.
The last look of a cloud leaving the hill behind.
Ourselves making little of it,
turning back to the work of tomorrow.

The years of my soul have come to this
chill morning in a long bed.
Under a duvet of sunlight or snow,
is there strength enough in ankle and thigh
down narrow paths to go?

Mora Maclean

PLAYING SCARECROW

It's tugged my gaze
back to a spot: at first
barely there, just
enough to stand
out: a blot, something black –
is it cross-shaped? – propped
up in a field, made bold
to be seen sprung
from the undulating green.

On the scan of horizon
another appears –
this time clear
as a boy; a joker popped
up in a crucifixion of joy,
in a stance that says
'Look – no hands!',
though he stands as still
rooted in the ground.

On this island
of holdings strewn, with solid rock
blown to ruin, it's a thought,
wind-borne, that is sewn and he's
shot up all over, full-grown,
his crossed 't's dotting the eyes,
in no time come of age.

In only
the tatters he's stood in, he weathers,
unchanging, the play
of all season and light;
the covering dark
shows him steadfast:
his memory bearing the night.

Bound to the days
blowing through him,
the skies fleeting over
his head;
is he blind
to how it haunts me –
this larking up a storm:
each cross the boundless reach of his
begging to be born?

Or is it – he's sighted
the mother, this once,
to mirror his circumstance:
for distance has blanked out the face;
she must wear her heart wide
                                        holding out
arms to embrace.

IN THE FITTING ROOM

The salesgirl talked me into this
tangle of sleeves, these sideways
Hitler salutes; trying jeans
that have me hopping to a tune.

The frock I seemed made for
has stitched me up, now hems me in;
I back out to find myself
in the midst of eight others:

all wearing my dress, each
a different angle on me;
one's twirling round, another
turns on bare heels, decided

she won't wear it, knows
how she feels. The salesgirl
appears: 'How we getting on?'
she asks my spitting images.

I answer for them;
for who wears the trousers
when it comes to straps and zips?
Who fastens the clips?

The dresser of them all,
capriciousness can strip them
just as quick, my departure
send them back to non-existence.

Yet they return: reflections
of selves I need to see.
One day I'll smash their faces,
swear I'll still walk out as me.

Tony McLean

F.FWD

Ever since I could remember I wanted a fast forward machine. I hated waiting. Life just seemed too slow.

My first memory is of waiting outside the close in Castlemilk for my maw to let me in for Paul's birthday party. Nobody else was back from school yet and I was standing with Brian Gould, hiding my face in the Coulter's hedge to avoid contact with his breath. He'd rotten breath. The whole Gould family'd rotten breath. I don't think their maw bought toothpaste, couldn't afford it. **F.FWD**

Stephen Gould's birthday party. Pieces with butter and sugar and fizzy orange that rotted the teeth. This was luxury for them, this was a party. **F.FWD**

Waking up in the dark. Cornflakes with milk that had frozen on the step. Walking to school past the Mitchellhill flats ever vigilant for Dominic O'Brien and his brick-chucking right arm. School – maths, school – reading, school – mass, school – staring out the window. Home – Scooby Doo – mince, doughballs and mashed potatoes – Tom and Jerry – in bed lying awake for hours. **F.FWD**

My maw making macaroon bars out of mashed potatoes and icing sugar. The whole house stinking of it for hours. **F.FWD**

Waking up in the dark. Porridge. Dodging bottles passing the high flats. School – staring out the window at the Bunsen burners up at the Grange secondary and telling the teacher that it was on fire. Home – Wacky Races and Stop The Pigeon – stew – Tom and Jerry – in bed lying awake listening to everyone outside collecting wood and stuff for the bonnie. **F.FWD**

Waking up in the dark. Golden Nuggets. Avoiding pish-filled balloons up at the high flats. School – special mass for Father Conlan. Having to walk past the coffin and seeing him as dead as... Rip trousers falling. Home. Belt belt, Scholl sandal across the arse. 'Get tae bed and wait till yer daddy gets in!' Starving and scared. Waiting, waiting and waiting. Paul coming into the room and belting me on the arm and calling me a lucky sod cause my da was on overtime. Waiting till tomorrow, same time same place, tune in. **F.FWD**

Fighting with Paul and Stuart to get to lick the mixing bowl that my maw rattled up the Fairy Cakes in. **F.FWD**
Getting up on Christmas morning at three o'clock. Wanting the day to last forever, but it flies in. Whoosh. **F.FWD**
School holidays lasting forever. Getting sent to Colchester and having to work at the surrounding farms. Pea picking, strawberry picking, tattie howking. Slave labour whatever way you looked at it. They farmers would've had us up the lum if they thought they could get away with it. **F.FWD**
Breaking a window in the conservatory. Skelp skelp. Paul breaking the branch of a hundred-year-old tree. Skelp skelp. Shiting it from their mad dog and sneakily eating the chocolate buttons that had been bought for the bloody thing. They tasted fine to us. **F.FWD**
Firing a sharp pencil at Stuart and narrowly missing his eye. Double doin from my maw. Don't – skelp – you – skelp – know – skelp – that – skelp – your – skelp – Nana – skelp – and – skelp – pappy – skelp – are – skelp – blind –skelp – because –skelp – of – skelp – clowns –skelp – like – skelp – you – SKELP. The final belt was always the fiercest, up until then she'd just been warming to her task, getting into the swing. I remember thinking what a bad bastard I must be, all the blind people in the world living in darkness because of me and my sharp pencils. **F.FWD**
Playing moshie with my da's medal he got from Cyprus cause I didn't have any coins to play with. Losing it to Robert Prentice. Sinking into the settee every time my da wondered where he'd put it. **F.FWD**
Moving to Erskine and having to wear a school uniform for the first time and feeling like a dick. Wondering why I was at school. Wondering why nobody ever told me. Fighting on the first day with Ross Moyer cause I threw a tennis racket at him. Hitting Joe McNally cause he wouldn't give me a shot on his bike. Fighting with anybody at all for any reason whatsoever. **F.FWD**
Not getting into the football team cause I'd no boots. **F.FWD**
Going to secondary. Different uniform same thought. Why was I at school? Not having a clue about anything. Not getting into the football team cause I'd no boots. Suffering from déjà vu. **F.FWD**

Having to shower with the second years. My da getting a job and me getting football boots. Getting into the team and scoring an own goal within five minutes of the start of my first game. Bounce, bounce. Ball flies over goalkeeper Pandy's flailing arms from a backward header from Baw Jaws at the half way line. Everybody shouting, me laughing. **F.FWD**

Every Tuesday the house'd be ram-packed with reject chocolate biscuits that my maw brought home from the factory she worked in. Every Friday we'd get interrogated by my da cause we'd scoffed the lot. Even the ones they'd planked. We could smell a chocadooby bikkie at a mile radius. **F.FWD**

Getting asked out by Gillian Galbraith and being too scared to say aye. Living in a family of boys I was scared and embarrassed in front of women. **F.FWD**

Hanging around with Ross Moyer and watching him get into at least a fight a week. **F.FWD**

Swimming in the Clyde among the johnnies and turds in the summertime. Walking around for miles and miles cause the only other thing to do was swim in the bloody Clyde! **F.FWD**

Wanting to ask out girls but still being too awkward. Going to community centre discos in Bishopton steaming, knowing that by the end of the night Ross'd be outside lamping somebody. All the while I was infatuated with Dot Walker and I'd ask Joe for the tenth time to ask her if she'd get off with me. For the tenth time she'd laugh and say nae chance. Getting outside and looking for the big crowd that would be surrounding Ross and this week's victim, wondering who it was. *'Tonight Matthew I will be beating up Pandy.' 'Oh terrific! Ladies and gentlemen, a big hand for Ross Moyer as tonight he beats up Pandy.'* He'd always win. He wasn't big; he wasn't strong; just determined. Hoping that nobody would jump in and hauner Ross's victim cause then me and Joe'd have to do likewise. **F.FWD**

Getting into the gas and thinking how fantastic it was that it only cost seventy odd pence. The buzz would last all night but by the time you went home your old dears were none the wiser. Straight as a die, not like when you go home with a drink in you, falling in doors and clambering over

chairs and plants that used to come at you out the blue. With butane you were stone cold. Stone cold. **F.FWD**
    Pappy getting taken into hospital. Dead within a week. Not realising what the hell was happening. No more wandering minds. No more 'where's ma teeth?' No more chap chap chapping at dominoes. No more whistling hearing aids. Carrying the coffin the wrong way round while wearing trousers that were too loose with no belt. Hoping they wouldn't fall down on the walk to the hearse. Never having seen so many blind folk in the one place before. Tap, tap, white stick, white stick. Lots of grey. Too much grey. **F.FWD**
    Failing O Grades. Getting drunk and swimming in the Clyde just for old times sake. Joe caught dysentery or something. Shiting and puking green. We were certain it wasn't the Callie Special. Ross leaving school and joining the Navy. I still wasn't even sure why I was there. **F.FWD**
    Career advice from my da. 'Here son I've seen ye've been dismantling yer stereo, ye don't fancy tryin yer haun at the auld electrician game, dae ye?' Big Joe just looked on perplexed as his live wire son managed to shock himself once more. **F.FWD**
    'Here son, whit if Ah teach ye tae drive and ye get yerself a job on the open road. Plenty ey freedom an ye're yer ain boss?' He listened from the bottom of the stairs as once more I crashed from the top. Couldn't even control my feet. **F.FWD**
    'Whit aboot gaun tae uni like yer brother? Get yerself a degree and the world's yer oyster.' Big Joe reaching into the cupboard under the sink for the calamine lotion as once more son # 2 comes in from sunbathing in the back garden looking like a lobster. **F.FWD**
    Getting a job in the butcher's and losing touch with everybody I was at school with. Hearing all the news second hand from Missus Bone Fur the Soup. 'Pandy killed himself,' she says in one breath. 'Oh, and four square slice,' she chirps in another. Poor sod walked into the Clyde, too scared of heights to chip himself from the bridge. **F.FWD**
    Then there was Mister Little Bit Of Mince For The Cat. 'Ah see that Dot Walker got married to that so-an-so whose brother got done for the drunk driving,' he snides out

the side of one cheek, 'Had to. Quarter of corned beef,' he says out the other. **F.FWD**

Finally there was the queen of the Erskine gossip scene, Missus Price Ey Totties. 'That's that Ross Moyer away tae the Falklands,' she laughs. 'Best place fur a daft lump like that.' She grabs her shopping bag tighter to her chest. 'And half a pound of that.' She nods aggressively at the stew. **F.FWD**

Lives turned into tittle-tattle. Important snippets of information traded across the counter. That was somebody I knew dead, another had broken my heart and the third getting sent to die. I made a mental note never to tell anyone my most intimate secrets. They would just be turned into sordid gossip, tomorrow's fish supper wrappers. It wasn't even time to close for lunch! I hated the adult world. **F.FWD**

Love hits you. Real love. Adult love. Like sticking your hand in a fire. Wee Karen. I couldn't see myself ever being without her. What would be the point of carrying on? Might as well follow Pandy into the Clyde. Suddenly you feel really grown up *and* childish at the same time. You can't hide your emotions, holding hands and kissing in public. **F.FWD**

In the local with Karen doing the pop quiz, kissing for every answer we got right when I see Ross Moyer. He looks the same but acts different. 'Went away to war,' he says. 'Came home and that Bev I was seeing's shacked up with Rab McLeod. I thought about kicking his head in, but I didn't want to give her the satisfaction of knowing that I was upset.' I feel his forehead. Is this the same Ross? The same Ross that could knock Rab McLeod into the same time next week. The same time next week next year! It was. The Navy made a man of him, turned him into a pacifist. Too scary. **F.FWD**

London lights call. Wee Karen gets a job and you follow down on her coat-tails. Living together. Sex on tap? Get a job as a security guard and feel as though I've been sent back to school again. Some clown inspecting my shiny shoes and how straight my clip-on tie was. Nightmare. The romance soon turns sour. Her eyes get dazzled by the lights and her exciting job. Mines are shut, hoping that the whole thing's just a bad dream. She hates my negativity. Chucked.

Dumped. Rubbered. Scorned. Spurned. Getting the Spanish Archer. Getting custody of the thesaurus. **F.FWD**

Getting made to feel childish again. Everybody else in the world's in a relationship except for me. Take up smoking just for the sake of it. It's what you do when you get put under pressure. **F.FWD**

Go and live in Cheltenham with Joe. Take up drinking as a profession. The years just fly by and the weight falls off. Pessimism has me by the balls. Forklift driver carrying aluminium bars about all day. If I'd've got breathalysed that would've been it. Jotters. **F.FWD**

After years of staggering love belts me again. Scabby Susie, barmaid in the local. Mad-as-a-paintbrush artist. I was sure this time this was it. This was me and her and a house on the hill, two weans and a dog to kick when things got rough. Who could ask for anything more? She covers my negativity and pessimism in a soft blanket of love. Give up the drink and pay off the debts. A couple of years later she fancies a move to Glasgow. I drop everything – Joe included – and hit the M6. I'd never had so much love. I'd no job, but what did it matter? **F.FWD**

However. I woke this morning and I'd been sleeping way out to the right and there was Susie, way out to the left.

I looked under the quilt and her sideways backside smiles at me. I knew then it wouldn't be long until I was once more wondering whether I was really cut out for this world of relationships. The old heave-ho's on its way. I thought for a second, blinked and wished for a quick **F.FWD** to get it over and done with. No acrimony, no bitterness, just a whoosh. But it made me think. Do I really want to fast forward? Is that not just a fast track to the grave? I realise that I no longer want a fast forward machine. It's a rewind loop I'm looking for now. Something that'll give me time to look around at my surroundings and allow me some time to think, some time to enjoy my life. **LOOP**

'By the way miss, why exactly am I at school?' **LOOP**

'Aye, I will go out with you, Gillian Galbraith.' **LOOP**

'Pandy! Come away from the edge of the water and stop being a stupid sod.' **LOOP**

'Naw, I don't fancy buzzing some butane.' **LOOP**

'Here Dot, it's obvious to me that you fancied Joe. Steam in, don't mind my feelings, I'll get over it.' **LOOP**

'Thanks for chucking me Karen, it's the right thing to do. Naw, naw, I'm not going to take up smoking.' **LOOP**

'Listen Joe. You've been a great mate and all that, but I'm just nipping up the M6 with Susie here. See ye soon.' **LOOP**

Etcetera. **LOOP**

Etcetera. **LOOP**

LOOP

    LOOP

        LOOP

That's the way forward, backwards. We learn from the lessons that our history teaches us.

Niall MacRath

DH'ÈIRICH SNATHAG
A MEADOW PIPIT ROSE UP

A-mach dhan a' chùl-cinn –
Out to the common grazing –
Bha na dianagan ri mì-mhàthaireachd a-rithist –
The gimmers were mis-mothering again –
'S mi a' leantainn beucail uain,
While following a lamb's bellowing,
Dh'èirich snathag ri mo thaobh;
A meadow-pipit arose just beside me;
Chaidh mi a dh'fhaicinn agus
I went to look, and
Siud nead àlainn fo bhadan fraoich.
There was this beautiful little nest under a clump of heather.
Ceithir uighean ballach, seasgair, blàtha,
Four speckled eggs, nestling warmly
Thug orm smaointinn air na bha.
Made me think about times long gone.

Cò mheud làithean a chuir mi seachad
How many days did I spend
Sna làithean geala (cha b' ann an-dè),
In far-off youth (it wasn't yesterday!),
Air leithid a mhonadh;
On moors like this one;
Bhithinn daonnan nam aonar
Always on my own
A' sireadh neadan.
Looking for nests.
Ach san àm sin b' e *whaup* an guilbneach,
But at that time curlews were whaups,
Pee-weep a' churracag; na *laverocks* os mo chionn
Lapwings were pee-weeps; laverocks over my head
Agus cha b' e an uiseag.
And not skylarks.
Cha robh guth air a' ghobhar-adhair;
Snipe were unheard of;
Chan fhacas boillsgeadh dhen a' bhrù-gheal.
Wheatears were never glimpsed.

Cha deach leam sna lorgan sin;
I didn't succeed in the searches;
Cha robh annam na dh'fhòghnadh de dh'fhoighidinn.
I just wasn't patient enough.
An-diugh, dh'amaisinn air rud sam bith
Today, I can turn my hand to anything
Ach bheirinn an saoghal
But I would give the world
Agus na tha air uachdar
And everything it contains
A bhith air ais air na monaidhean cèine
To be back on those far-off moors
Aig toiseach mo shiubhail.
At the start of my journey.
(Ach rèitich mi dianag is uan).
(But I reunited gimmer with lamb).

TOBHTA RUAIRIDH A' GHLINNE
RORY OF THE GLEN'S RUINED HOUSE

Tha gleann beag dìomhair a-bhos againne,
There is a small secret glen near here
Thall air cùl a' chùl-cinn;
Out beyond the common grazing;
Agus air cùl gaoithe, 's ri aghaidh grèine,
And sheltered from wind, and facing the sun
Tha Tobhta Ruairidh a' Ghlinne.
Is Rory of the Glen's ruined house.

Chithear bàthach, àth is buaile,
Byre, cornkiln and cowfold can still be seen,
Talamh torrach aoil is uisge bho eas.
Fertile lime-rich soil, and water was from a waterfall.
A' choirc a' fàs sna h-achannan beaga shìos;
The oats growing in the small fields below;
A' bhanachag òg a' seinn aig tràth eadraidh –
The milkmaid singing at milking time –
Agus feasgar, dol-fodha na grèine sa Chuilthionn.
And of an evening, sunset over the Cuillins.
An ann mar sin a bha ur cuibhreann?
Was that your lot?

No an aithneachadh sibh mo chas-sa
Or would you recognise the state I'm in
Is cion-iùil mo bheatha;
And my directionless life;
Nuair a thigeadh an geamhradh
When winter came
An do leagadh ur spiorad gu làr?
Did your spirit hit rock-bottom?
Dh'fhàg sibh an gleann
You left the glen
Tha na h-achannan fo luachair.
The fields are rush-covered.

Lyn Moir

NOT AN EIDER DUCK

floating aimlessly in the ebbing drift,
a black and white symmetrical affair,
abandoned football, bobbing to one side
first, among the fishing boats, then towards
the other, almost beaching on the sand
and rock, then lurching up against the wall,
green growth uncovered where the water slips
inexorably down. I'd thought it was
too passive for an eider, too spherical,
too dead, too high above the waterline.
Dead seabirds do not float like ballcocks loosed
to make their pilgrimage to sea, they sink.

Michael Munro

TIME FOR NEW STORIES

Saw you standing in the subway
your hair rough-lifted by the subterranean wind.
I willed you:
put yourself into my hands,
let this decision take itself
unnoticed
and not any other now.
Days rattled by like subway trains
and years went round and round again.
You kissed me though your tooth was sore
and cloves erupted in my mouth
like kissing Christmas.
By such and such
our lives mythologise.

Donald S. Murray

HATS

They bestowed free religion on all heads,
these products of Protestant hat factories:
a sales assistant's whispered tête-à-tête
telling them that coming complimentary
with their exchange of money for a hat
– whether homburg, cloth cap or trilby –
came a headful of the type of mind that
forced them to consider theology's
finer points; how whistling and singing tried
God's love and patience on the Sabbath day
or how the horned one Lucifer might alight
on a ceilidh dance to steal men's souls away.

To women, too, a haberdashery
in which God's every secret was unstitched.
With each pill-box or bonnet came a free
promise of Paradise's great riches,
vouchsafed to those who flowered among pews
and yet denied to turban-circled heads.
the mitre or biretta-wearing few
who by a skull-capped celibate were led,
the wimpled nun, yarmulka-crowned Jew,
Egyptian with a kaffiyeh or fez,
for Heaven's gates are only unlocked to
those wearing Free Kirk headgear on this earth.

Siùsaidh NicRath

A' CHOINNEAMH

Bha i fadalach. Phut i an doras agus chaidh i a-steach. Bha e cho soilleir a-muigh air an t-sràid agus cho dorcha a-staigh. Sheas i airson greis gus an do dh'fhàs a sùilean cleachdte ris an dorchadas. Beag bho bheag thòisich a h-uile càil a' tighinn am follais dhi, na bùird bheaga le anart smlach; soirean le ròs singilte, gun uisge, plastaig; an solas lag bho choinneil no dhà a' priobadh anns an dubhar; dealbhan de rionnagan, fada marbh 's fada mu làr. Mar as àbhaist bha an seòmar falamh. Uill, bha Seac ann, bha esan an còmhnaidh ann, ach cha robh esan a' cunntadh. Bha e mar phìos àirneis, gun anam, na sheasamh air cùl bùird-malairt, aparan fada geal air 's a mhuinichillean trusaichte. Uaireannan shaoileadh i nach b' urrainn dha bruidhinn ann. Cha robh i air a ghuth a chluinntinn riamh.

Sheall i ris. Bha esan a' coimhead oirre, 's an uair sin chrom e a cheann dhan oisean. Cha d' rinn i gàire, cha tuirt i smid. An àite sin, leig i osna aiste, thionndaidh i agus chaidh i tarsainn an t-seòmair le ceum mall. Bha iad a' suidhe daonnan anns an oisean ud, far an robh am bòrd leis fhèin, ballachan timcheall air a dh'fhalaicheadh iad bhon t-saoghal. Shuidh i air a' bheing, 's shrùc an glùinean ri chèile. Ghabh iad grèim air an làmhan os cionn a' bhùird 's theannaich iad ri chèile iad cho cruaidh 's gun do dh'fhàs iad goirt. An toiseach b' àbhaist dhaibh a bhith a' cumail an làmhan fon bhòrd air eagal 's gum faiceadh duine iad.
Ach cha robh adhbhar ann sin a dhèanamh. Cha do chuir duine riamh dragh orra.

– *Tha mi duilich, bha...bha e doirbh.* Bha a guth fann 's làn bròin.
– *Ist, coma leat.*
Chaidh a làmh a chumail cho teann 's gun do thòisich a fàinne ga gearradh. Mar as trice chuireadh i dhith i ach bha i air dìochuimhneachadh an-diugh.

Bha an t-àite cho sàmhach. An-dràsta 's a-rithist thigeadh srann cuileig-mòire, air a thighinn beò tràth leis a' ghrèin laig

is gealladh an earraich. Thug i sùil chun na h-uinneige bhon robh an srann a' tighinn. Bha a' chuileag a' fàs drochnàdarrach agus beagan eu-dòchasach, a' feuchainn ri faighinn a-mach. Bha e coimhead cho furasta ach cha robh. Rinn i osna a-rithist.
Tron uinneig b' urrainn dhi saoghal eile fhaicinn, daoine ann an cabhaig, daoine a' cabadaich, daoine a' gàireachdainn, clann a' ruith, coin a' comhartaich, trafaig. Ach cha b' urrainn dhi càil a chluinntinn. Bha e neònach, mar a bhith a' coimhead air telebhisean gun fhuaim.

Sheall i ris a' choinneil agus anns an t-solas aice bha a h-aodann coltach ri aon de na dealbhan air a' bhalla, aodann cho bàn taibhseach, a shùilean dubha mar gu robh iad air buillean fhaighinn. Bha i air chrith ged nach robh e fuar. Chan robh fios aice dè bu chòir dhi a ràdh. Bha i a' dol a bhruidhinn ach an uair sin, smaoinich i, Dè math? Thàinig a' cheist nach robh i ag iarraidh a chluinntinn.
– An do dh'innis thu fhathast dhà?

Thòisich a' chuileag-mhòr a-rithist, faisg oirr', cho faisg 's gun saoileadh i gun robh i na ceann. Cha b' urrainn dhi smaoineachadh. Sguab i air falbh i le cais.
Bha an t-sàmhchair do-ghiùlainte. Thàinig a' cheist a-rithist.
– An do dh'innis thu dhà? An do dh'innis thu dha mar deidhinn?

Bha a' cheist air chrith eatarra, trom, dòchasach anns an t-sàmhchair os cionn na coinnle. Bha i a' faireachdainn lapach, 's bha a beul tioram. Bha i a' feuchainni ri bruidhinn, bha a bilean a' gluasad ach cha tàinig facal. Bha an srann air tòiseachadh a-rithist, fad às, ach a' tighinn na b' fhaisge, a' chuileag ag itealaich mun cuairt, a' feuchainn ri faighinn a-mach. Agus an uair sin thàinig faclan eile, ann an guth ìosal.
– Gheall thu dhomh. A-raoir, thuirt thu e. Tha gaol agad ormsa. Tha fhios a'm. Tha thu gad mhealladh fhèin.
Bha an guth a' sainnseareachd.

Bha a ceann goirt 's rinn i ùrnaigh, – O, Dhè, cuidich mi. Bha a' choinneal a' priobadaich, air chrith, gu dol às. Deur-shùileach, dh'èirich i 's ruith i tron t- seòmar 's a-steach don

A' CHOINNEAMH

taigh-bheag. Chrom i a ceann air beulaibh an sgàthain, a làmhan air a' bhalla agus dh'fhuirich i ann an sin, dìreach mar sin gus an do sguir na deòir a' ruith bho a sùilean. Bha an sgàthan fuar air a h-aodann agus bha i a' faireachdainn na b' fhèarr 's na bu chiùine. Sheas i a' smaoineachadh. 'S e an fhìrinn a th' ann, smaoinich i, tha mi gam mhealladh fhìn. Tha mi a' tuigsinn sin a-nis. 'S ann dall a bha mi, cho dall. Fàgaidh mi e.

B' urrainn dhi a h-aodann fhaicinn anns an sgàthan agus bha gàire beag air. Chuir is suathag luath no dhà air a h-aodann is rinn i air an t-seòmar eile.

Bha Seac na sheasamh ri taobh an dorais fhosgailte agus solas is fuaim an latha a-muigh a' dòrtadh a-steach. Bhruidhinn e.
– *Ro fhadalach*, thuirt e rithe. – *Tha ise air falbh*.

AINMHIDH

Chaidh i suas an staidhre. Cha do chuir i an solas air ged a bha e glè dhorch. Cha d' rinn i fuaim idir air ceann a stocainnean is bha fios aice air a h-uile step co-dhiù, is dè 'n fheadhainn a bha dìosgadh. Bha e anmoch, faisg air uair sa mhadainn. Bha e na cleachdadh aice bho chionn bhliadhnaichean a bhith dol innte anmoch. Bhiodh an duine aice a' dol suas aig deich uairean no na bu thràithe agus bhiodh an t-sàmhchair a' còrdadh rithe as dèidh dha a dhol suas. 'N uair sin shuidheadh i ri taobh an teine na h-aonar agus dheidheadh i thairis air na rudan a bha air tachairt air feadh an latha, no thar nam bliadhnachan, no air feadh a beatha fhèin air fad. Uaireannan dhèanadh i norrag agus uaireannan eile leughadh i leabhar. Cha robh esan air leabhar a leughadh riamh.

Bha an taigh glè shàmhach. Cha robh dad ri chluinntinn ach srannail shocair an duine aice a' tighinn às an t-seòmar-cadail aca. Leig i osna nuair a chuala i sin. Bha i an-còmhnaidh taingeil nuair a bha e na chadal. Chuir i a h-aodach dhith le cabhaig is tharraing i gùn-oidhche oirre. 'N uair sin shiolp a-steach i gu faicealach dhan leabaidh air an taobh aice fhèin. Lean esan air a' srannail.

Dhùin i a sùilean is dh'fheuch i ri chadal. Rinn i osann eile. Mar as motha a dh'fheuchadh i ri cadal, 's ann as motha a bha e faileachadh oirre. Bha i a' smaoineachadh air an leabaidh fhèin, is an dithis aca a-nis cùl ri cùl aig an oirean fhèin den leabaidh. Bha caolas mòr air fàs eatarra thar nam bliadhnachan, caolas cho mòr 's gu robh e mar chuan a-nis is iadsan a' fuireach air dà thaobh a' chaolais seo, mu choinneamh a chèile 's gun fiù 's an aon chànan aca.

Bha i air chrith leis an fhuachd ag èisteachd anns an dorchadas ris na cùirtearan a bha placadh an-dràsta 's a-rithist aig an uinneig mar bhratach brònach. Chùm i a sùilean dùinte gu teann is thòisich i a' smaoineachadh air làithean blàtha samhraidh nuair a bha i òg is i fhèin 's a piuthar nan laighe air a' mhachair is a' ghrian os an cionn is iad a' spleuchdadh suas dhan speuran gorma a' feuchainn ri na h-uiseagan fhaicinn.

B' urrainn dhaibh an ceilearadh a chluinntinn agus

dh'èireadh an t-òran tiamhaidh le dannsa nan eun, 'n uair sin thuiteadh e, dh'èireadh e a-rithist is thuiteadh e. Cha mhòr nach robh e mar analachadh fhèin is rinn an cuimhneachadh an dà chuid a blàthachadh agus a sòlasachadh gus an do thuit i na cadal.

Bha a' ghaoth air a bhith ag èirigh is chuala i fuaim a bha fad às an toiseach air sgàth 's nach robh i cinnteach dè bh' ann. Gu slaodach, thàinig e thuice gur e an geata a bha a' bragail leis a' ghaoith an-dràsta 's a-rithist agus mar a b' fhaide a dh'èist i, 's ann a b' àirde chaidh am fuaim gus mu dheireadh gun tug e oirre èirigh. Gu luath, ruith i shìos an staidhre, a' toirt mionnan dhan duine aice. Bhiodh e an-còmhnaidh a' dìochuimhneachadh an geata a dhùnadh às a dhèidh is bha i seachd searbh dhe na caoraich a' tighinn a-staigh is ag ithe a h-uile dìthean is lus a bha sa ghàrradh aice.

Tharraing i bòtannan oirre anns an trannsa, is rug i air a' bhiùgan is dh'fhosgail i an doras. Cha robh sgeul air a' ghealaich is e cho dubh ris an t-sùith a-muigh is bha soillse a' bhiùgain bhig cho lag 's nach mòr gum bu lèir dhi an staran. Gu faicealach rinn i a slighe chun a' gheata, a' cumail a sùilean air an talamh. Cheangail i e le pìos ròpa is thionndaidh i 'n uair sin is thòisich i a' dol air ais chun an taighe. Mus d' ràinig i e, chuala i fuaim a chuir cais oirre. 'Ro fhadalach!', smaoinich i, 'tha na caoraich a-staigh mar thà.' Stiùir i am biùgan far an robh am fuaim is chunnaic i sùilean a' deàrrsadh anns an leth-sholas fhann. Cha b' e caora a bh' ann idir.

Nuair a bha i òg, bu neònach leatha gum biodh eagal air cuid de dhaoine ro dhamhain-allaidh no ro shealladh fala is eagal air feadhainn eile ro àitean àirde no ro luchagan. Ach cha robh eagal oirre-se ro na rudan sin riamh, ise a shreapadh a' chraobh a b' àirde no a ghearradh amhaich muilt gun smaoineachadh mu dheidhinn. Ach ro na creutairean sin, aon dhiubh a bha a-nis na sheasamh eadar i-fhèin is sàbhailteachd, bha eagal air a bhith oirre fad a beatha. Cha robh fios no cuimhne aice carson.

Gu dearbh, dh'fhaodadh i aideachadh gur e creutairean uasal, eireachdail, cumhachdach a bh' annta nam biodh iad fad air falbh bhuaipe no mura biodh i na h-aonar. Ach dlùth orra no na h-aonar, bhiodh eagal a beath' aice rompa. Cha robh iad uasal ach uabhasach is cha robh iad eireachdail ach eagalach is cha robh iad cumhachdach ach cunnartach. Bhiodh fios aca, dh'fhairicheadh iad gun robh eagal oirre is b' urrainn dhaibh sealltainn troimhpe agus an oillt a bha na laighe mu cridhe fhaicinn. Bha iad cho làidir is ise cho lag is bha sin a' còrdadh riutha.

Ach a-nis anns an dorchadas cha b' urrainn dhi gluasad, cha b' urrainn dhi fiù 's anail a tharraing. Reòthte, na seasamh air an staran, a gùn-oidhche a' crathadaich mu a casan is am biùgan briste far an robh e air tuiteam air an talamh. Bha a h-aodann fliuch. Mas e sileadh nan speur no sileadh nan sùl a bh' ann, cha robh fios aice agus shìn i a làmhan a-mach roimpe mar neach a bha dall.

B' urrainn dhi a chluinntinn ged nach b' urrainn dhi fhaicinn tro a sùilean dùinte ach chuala i na fuaimean snotrach, smotach sin a bha aig an còmhnaidh ga cur à cochall a cridhe is a thug gris oirre is iad a' tighinn na b' fhaisge is na b' fhaisge. Thug i oirre fhèin a sùilean fhosgladh is chunnaic i aodann is a shùilean a' coimhead oirre. Nuair a bhean e rithe, ghabh i uiread de dh'fheagal 's gun do tharraing i anail mhòr a thug air ais a guth. Leig i sgread aiste, dh'èigh i a-mach, 'Na str'cc annams', na strùc annam!' is dh'fheuch i air le na buillean. Chuir an sgread is am bualadh stad air is a' leigeil grìosad às, ghluais e air ais gu a thaobh aige fhèin den leabaidh.

Bha na cùirtearan fhathast a' placadaich ris an uinneig is an geata a' bragail leis a' ghaoith.

Chris Powici

EWE SKULL

between the curlew's nest
and moor stream's stony rush
this small white death;

faded radiance of fox-licked bone
sunk in ling and flecked by spits of rain
drifting inland on a faint sea-wind

Sarah Reynolds

THE VISITORS

He sits in the garden, waiting. Waiting and waiting for time to roll over him, for ninety-one summers to become ninety-three, ninety-four...

He says, 'I know your face lassie... and yours,' and, 'is that a wee bird or a leaf?'

He says, 'They're nice enough to you here. It's a lovely day.'

We watch together, the three of us. We watch the sky move and the trees sway and the boy in the mower hum in and out of the beds and shrubs leaving billiard green grass behind him.

We say, 'Are you comfortable here – is the food good?'

He says, 'They're nice enough to you,' then hesitates, kneading at the knitted tammy in his lap with one hand, soothing the curved neck of his cane with the other. His fingers become slower and slower on the marled wool. He is reading it. 'I don't know where she went. All dressed in frills and that, I don't know why she would be all dressed up like that. I kissed her... and, I cuddled her. She went down like a bag of potatoes. I wish it was me.'

No-one has any words. There are Livingston daisies laughing in the borders. Redwood trees like rocket ships keeling further towards you the longer and harder you look up. Clamouring birdsong, a Red Admiral flirting in and out of the roses.

'I don't know what she had to go and do that for.'

His shirt is all faded to winter, open over a clean vest. Once it was vivid – royal blue with crimson tramlines. His pockets are torn, the buttons broken. His belt is hauled tight, holding him up.

'I know your face.'

'We brought you a wee half-bottle, Papa. And some biscuits.'

'Oh aye. You needn't have bothered with me. I like a wee snifter though. There's a bottle in my room, it's still got that much in it.' He gestures two inches. 'I know your...'

'I'm your granddaughter!' I repeat, too quickly, too loudly, too much angst in my voice. I gush on, talking

desperate rubbish, and at the mention of a dog he lights up. The dog leads him to everything – names, faces, cars, places. Those who visit, those who don't, the people he never talks to and the woman who sings all the time.
'She's a bloody nuisance, her.' He grins. The grin is meddling, young.

Snakes in the grass and bloody nuisances, me and my brother in a lost world of grand-childhood, combing beaches and his patience. Salt wind in our faces and a dizzy sky, we slip and slither on the rocks in stout Clark's sandals and his hands keep us from falling off the edge of the world. Gran on a striped fold-down chair with her knitting needles clicking, keeping watch over shell-studded castles and moats. I can't be in this place any more.

When we make moves to go, he lifts his face for a kiss. And this man who used to lift me up to the clouds cannot lift himself from the chair. He shrugs our help away and we follow him under low ceilings and dull lights through a maze of empty armchairs. He stops to consider every turn, looking for clues to room 5. There's a reproduction case clock standing against the modern wall like a reluctant sentry. The pendulum swings without disturbing the peace. In the bedroom he points to a framed picture on his otherwise barren dressing table. The glass is cracked. He puts his tammy down next to it.

'Aw Mamie. Seventy years. Seventy years together and she goes down just like that. I've a house just down the road. I've a mind to go there... I think it's empty. I've a mind to go there but on your own, it's not the same. It's nice enough here.'

At the door we hear him tell the nurse that we were more of those visitors from Glasgow. There's nothing real outside but the sound of our feet on the gravel until we look at each other in the closed car. We touch.

'He's looking well,' we say, and leave the air heavy with other thoughts.

On the road back to the motorway we pass the graveyard. I can't look round. I hold on to myself and say hello to her away in the back of my mind. I look down and my knuckles are white. I wonder where the clock from that house along the road went. I used to listen to its heartbeat in my tightly tucked bed.

I look up and the sky is blue on blue. Cloudless. I don't know why she had to go and do that either.

R.J. Ritchie

NEW WORDS – an abecedarium

amstelwort abreckon affletrush
breckle bamplosh bispremoceous
chirboule clintropholia clampephrobe
dorphin dillombrous dreftful
ebbramine eggaltump efflossiparous
flengible fomblish farkentoomery
gloysung gleesh gunderacious
hesquilline hardinjery hickertong
imbriche ispranulle instrod
josprang jellubrine jasstock
kentle kusselobery klebberty
lossbonney leckergentic lobsfuddle
mumberty moostril monjipene
nodgeralia norplestang naxentib
orklet oobladdation osprill
prectible punthersome pamplone
querdonic quallashe querbid
rumplery rassitous rungulascipple
splorish strumplety squandricle
troster thrope tortellise
umbrod uggerole ullicks
verdingle vosserith vanstrel
wheeblish wipplety wembertank
xerbocken xandertush xynophrenoppolist
yintlering yumber yipperade
zoaste zuberchack zerromberello

Lydia Robb

AUNTIE BEAN UNDRESSES

Her basement windae
chaps the street in twa;
faceless fowks' buits and shune
slaister throu rain.

She pous the chenille curtains an
like a moth emergin fae its chrysalis,
my auntie taks her claes aff,
sheddin the faulds like husks.

There's the sough o her taffeta blouse,
the reeshle o a lang black skirt,
the creak o her styes. Silk
stockins concertina roun her ankles.

I keek wi curious een fae in alow
the eiderdoon, but miss the slicht o haund,
the glisk o her saft breist,
Aa is nivir revealed.

Her neck tortoises throu the collar
o her winceyette gounie. There is
the warm smell o soap an sweit
an somethin indefinable.

ANTISYZYGY

Like a buzzard, he's gauging distances
between the crows atrophied on the fence
and the feral kitten comma'd on the midden.
I watch the old man watching me,
a shotgun slung across a freckled arm,
his stubbled face dour as his barren acres.
A yawnin gin trap frets at his feet,
its sharpened teeth honed in anticipation.
The morning air sours with the smell of slurry.
His boots sucking mud, he turns
towards the wood and some unseen quarry.
Late afternoon I catch him, hunkered
by the blackthorn. Nail half-mooned with dirt,
finger to lip, he motions.
A butterfly, wings trembling, settles on
his grazed knuckle. Colours bleed into light;
rainbow round a gold-ringed eye.
A Peacock Blue. He gestures, *First in years*
then shakes his head, allows himself a smile.

Kirsteen Scott

AT THE DANCE

I will hang words on a line
and they will shine
like glowworms
on a summer night

anchovy and bergamot,
crockery and dunce,
eglantine and flying fish,
greed and hunter's hill

and I will string them up
and watch them dance.

dodecahedron,
psalms and Pontefract
dither on the line

and little joining words
like and and but and though.

they are small word beetles,
wingless and intact,
glowing
as they wait

Robert Swift

THE PLAITED DOG-TURD WITH THE OAK-LEAF SAIL

There had been warning signs. Like the incident that morning when he had been cleaning his teeth. He'd spat into the basin and a globule of toothpaste (he always used too much), had fallen into the porcelain basin, shined up so white by Cath, and in the spat-up shining bead was a writhing creature; too many legs for an insect, but too limp for a woodlouse, though of course it was water-logged, so even hard casings might soften. Had he coughed it up from his stomach? Like that old woman in Nigeria who claimed to have vomited up a tortoise and had achieved a moment of tabloid fame? He rationalised that of course he hadn't. But where then had it come from? Had it sought refuge from the light in the tube of toothpaste, and been brushed around his mouth? Or fallen from the ceiling, maybe? He looked up, then rinsed it away, then wondered if he'd imagined it, but it was too late. Then, later, there was the dog-turd, beached on the pavement, and plaited, like a girl's pigtail. A mustard-coloured oak leaf, dried by the wind, rose from it like a sail. He'd bent to study it, and passers-by had glanced at him, but he'd had to check. Yes, perfectly plaited, or at least that's what he remembered of it, but things blur as soon as you turn away.

The eventide was blurred, slipping away to emptiness, like in an old movie. It was outside the car, but pressing in, getting closer. He could feel it creeping through the cavities and folds of his body. The opaque air hung in shifting grey layers among the fields, girding the trees which rose above it, their lower trunks half-submerged in the hushed dampness. He peered through the windscreen, on the lookout for the taillights of the next car. The hushed grey breath of the evening pressed against the car windows, clouding his senses. The margin of time, the spinning of the earth and the pull of the weak, dying, winter sun, combined to draw his eye time and again, for a piece of a second only, from the road. He felt disconnected from himself, and from the voice on the radio, coming somehow in unseen waves, with the illusion of substance.

He couldn't avoid it when it came, elegantly on tiptoes from the shadow of one of the gateways, its ears held erect. They're always larger than you remember from the time before, maybe because you compare them with rabbits, and like spirits with a hint of something human. It was very quick. The steering wheel shuddered as first the front wheels then the rear wheels struck the poor animal. Th-thum. He could feel the end of its life through the steering wheel, and he cried out and braked, but didn't stop. There could be no hope: Th-thum. The sensation he felt through the steering wheel stayed with him, the tremble of the hare's life, which he had taken, made him in turn tremble. The weather forecast on the radio told of the promise of sunshine to come the next day. He could see nothing in the rear mirror, but there could surely be no hope. In his mind he could see it, crouching in spring barley, in the sunshine, its bright, unblinking eyes, full of watchful wildness, the breeze ruffling its soft oatmeal fur. Then writhing in agony on the asphalt, smashed and oozing crimson blood onto the damp, hard, grey road metal. He slowed, almost to a stop, then drew away again, and tuned the radio to a light music station.

*

At home he and Cath watched the news, he swivelling in his special recliner, with his toes stretched towards the coal-effect gas fire. Dad's chair. The evening outside was gone from him now, and had given way to the domestic ritual, both tedious and comforting in its repetitions. The washing-up waited in the kitchen. They couldn't miss the news, which fed them like an intravenous placebo.

'How was your day, dear?' Not looking at him.

'Fine. Thanks. What about yours?'

'Oh, all right. Sammy fell off his bike, but it's just a graze. Jo went to the dentist. Needs a filling. She eats too many sweets. The window cleaner was in court for assaulting his wife last week. Seems such a nice man. I don't know who we'll get to clean the windows now. You never know about people do you?'

He wondered if she meant him.

'Have you noticed any woodlice about the house?'

'Woodlice?' Her inflexion was scathing. They wouldn't dare. 'I'll buy a spray if you like.'

He couldn't tell her about the hare. He kept thinking about it as he did the washing up. It was only a hare, he told himself. They ate lambs without a pang, and some folk ate hares. Jugged or something, whatever that meant. He dropped a mug, but it just bounced with a ringing sound. It's always the ones you don't like that don't break, he thought.

'What was that?' she called from the living room.

'Nothing.' Why does she have to know everything? Life would be more interesting if they had some secrets.

He couldn't sleep that night and got up for a drink of water. The mist had lifted, dispersed by breezes which disturbed the trees. He looked at the moon through the landing window, rising like the dead, unblinking eye of a blind man. It would be reflected off the bloodstained road: the dead touching the dead.

*

He took a different route next day, to attend a meeting in town before going to the office, but he came back home the usual way. He looked for the body, which by now would be a flattened furry rag, he thought. There were bunches of gaudy flowers in cellophane, like the ones you buy in filling stations from plastic buckets, next to the racks of newspapers. It didn't make sense. There was a teddy bear and other toys, in a pile by the road. Around the corner, where the road widened, there was a police car with a flashing light, two officers in luminous jackets shielding their eyes from the dazzle of his headlights. He stopped and wound down his window.

'Do you usually travel this road at this time of night, sir?'

But before he could answer the second officer called his colleague to the front of the car, pointing to the bumper, bent and dislodged.

He didn't know what they meant when they asked him about the child. He began telling them about the hare, speaking words that were not his own, till he broke down in tears: a child himself. As they talked over their radios the image that for a moment flickered before him, was of the plaited dog-turd with its oak-leaf sail.

Judith Taylor

AFTER SAPPHO (FRAGMENT 22)

I beg you:
show yourself.

Tonight again the air is close
with longing

and a glimpse of you
will earth that electricity
through whoever sees.
                            My

heart, shocked,
has taken on a life of its own:

I used to sneer
at the cult of love, but now

I wish

I pray.

CHICKEN POEM

Chickens with breeding.
Chickens with crests and fancy feathers.
Chickens with swagger and loud,
carrying voices. Chickens with bright, acquisitive eyes.
Chickens with claws
and pugilistic stances.
Chickens with attitude: chickens who know for a fact
the world's their dunghill.
Chickens with spurs.
Chickens with long, shiny cavalry boots
and scarlet jackets.
Chickens with tails
for evening wear; with brandies and big cigars.
Chickens with maps.
Chickens with shares in the railway-company. Chickens
   with trade concessions
and gunboats off the harbour.

Chickens with missions,
chickens with faith.
Chickens with only the best intentions.
Chickens with master plans
and a manifest destiny.
Chickens who want to forget
and chickens who can't go back 'til they're dead.
Chickens with Tennyson (*never*
Kipling – Kipling is vulgar) off by heart.
Chickens shooting at elephants;
shooting film
of the vanishing native customs.

Chickens who took the boat
and the chance of a whole new life; who took
the shilling; who took a place,
they believed, on high
amidst the gods of their chosen country.

All these chickens, who after
all these years, are making their way
back home.

Sheila Templeton

CALYX FOR GEORGIA O'KEEFFE

You sexy little thing. Georgia noticed you, half hidden,
coy in the back row of the wedding bouquet and slid
you out from the other stems. She carried you home,
all the way to her studio, to see to you. Stroke your
silky hood, drift fingertips down that snowy calyx
to your stamen tip, gorgeous in farm buttery yellow,
dusted in pollen and ready for anything.

You lucky thing. All these nerve endings under the skin,
enough of each gender to have your own bed bonanza.
No need to comb the New Mexico desert looking for a mate.
You have it all. Woman's parts petalled soft, swaddled,
parting for your little bit of man, ensuite, complete.
No wonder you were perfectly happy, standing perjink,
prim, listening to the first bars of the wedding march.

But Georgia spotted you. And here you are, sitting
in her favourite vase looking out at Taos mountain,
as she paints you into her life. Lingering over each line,
bringing known from unknown. Paying attention.
And, not content with that, set you up on curvy,
split tailed dolphins cavorting under your root.
     In case we'd somehow failed to get the message.

ROASTING VEGETABLES FOR LUNCH

We did the shopping first.
In Laiguelia market, the morning stretched
lazy arms. We stroked glossy purple aubergines,
held powdery-lilac swollen heads of garlic,
weighed single tomatoes. Each one
would have made a workman's lunch.

Then the slow walk home with string bags
criss crossing their raffia taut on creamy-brown
potatoes, like lace over a girl's slim thigh.
Back in the cool dark kitchen, we eased knots
of earth out of hidden places, sluicing skin
squeaky clean; trimmed and sliced, discarding
the unnecessary. Spread fresh butter,
green-golden olive oil, lapping, overlapping
layers, trusting the magic of alchemy;
which came, hot from the charcoal oven.

Well polished metal blackened with promise.
Sweet potatoes soft peachy orange. Onion hearts
milky silver glistening sweating garlic cloves crisped
melting inside stem courgettes cut lengthwise
gleaming carrots saffron coloured juices
browned butter and good olive oil smelling
of hot sun. Turnips yellow-orange gritty. Squash
quartered among crusted potatoes dipped in flour.

We taste and taste, crunching blackened twigs
of thyme and peppery marjoram to punctuate
all the soft flesh and juices running,
the pinky orange glistening on our skin.

Tim Turnbull

THE STOCKMAN'S CALENDAR

Four Northern Æclogues

Spring

The fields fill up with fresh, green grass and beasts, just
 recently released,
 who kick their heels in skittish dances.
Songbirds warble up the Eden valley; stake out their claims
 to territory
 balanced on the tips of branches

as I lie on my side and watch the Doctor Martens swagger off
 and when I move come rushing back.
Hormones and the rising of the sap are all that I can think
 provoked
 this unprovoked attack.

Summer

Frankie Valli issues from the disco as they leave. His shirt
 is stained with sweat.
 She's pretty in her summer dress.
The glass comes out of nowhere, smashes on his head and
 cuts his face and neck
 the flying splinters make a mess

of hers. She will, of course, be scarred for life. The pissed-
 up thug is quickly caught
 and his defence is a novel one.
The night was hot, he tells the court, and in the failing
 light he thought
 the couple were from Bridlington.

Autumn

He lies back in the dried-up ditch, stares at the haws and
    the harvest moon,
  and listens to the sound of the car.
He sees the lights flash through the hedge and knows that
    they are after him
  with baseball bats and iron bars.

At four a.m. he scrambles out and makes his dew-drenched
    way back home.
  Next year there is a big pub fight
and one of the gang gets killed. When he reads it he thinks
    it's sad, but still
  it serves the stupid bastard right.

Winter

The car park puddles are filmed with ice. The chestnut
    twigs are clacking in
  the bitter wind from out the east
and they've been drinking all afternoon and aren't in the
    mood for packing in
  just because serving time has ceased.

Next day not one of them can remember what happened to
    start the dispute
  but the doctor's skin was brown
so they drove like hell in hot pursuit, and gave him a taste
    of fist and boot
  when they caught him up at the edge of town.

Fiona Ritchie Walker

INSIDE THE KIST

Not even washed, so I know it was his doing.
When my mother died I buried combs and clasps
to make her ready for the journey.

My hands still smell of fish.
Last thing I remember was cooking,
him complaining of being hungry.

Who will feed my children?
Our only pan lying with me
in this cold stone kist.

A pan as thick as our axe,
though not as sharp,
but in his hands struck heavy.

There are dark stains on my shawl.
He will give her my best dress,
the one I should be wearing.

She will carry her pan to my house like a prize.
Soon she will find my salt and herbs,
know all my kitchen secrets.

GLACIER

She listens carefully to the instructions.
Use the ice axe, keep the rope taut,
never turn feet sideways.

She watches the rope stretch, hears dark slush
crunch beneath careful strides, a relentless rhythm,
the pull of those before and behind.

She wants to stop, to look at the ice,
the patches of pure glass,
that sea of frozen ripples.

Swirls of blue spiral down. She stretches to see
the bottom. The sun is widening the water lozenges,
she must watch where she is stepping.

Above, where blue meets blue,
a distant avalanche,
the top so unstable no-one can climb there.

Time to head down but first
one last upward look,
the rope pulling, crack deepening,

her wet stumble, ice
freezing skin,
a rush so loud

she cannot hear the others calling
through all those frozen colours.
Her very own kaleidoscope.

IMAGINING 90

The care staff call me Twiggy,
not that I'm thin. Oak tree thighs
and no waist. Straight after breakfast
I'm in the hall, carrier bags in pockets,
two steps, bend and pick.

The Inner Wheel took me out,
a drive in the country,
chance to revisit my roots.
I remembered the best spots
for collecting, clutched the bags
all the way home, stoked up
my open wardrobe, the match lit
before any of them twigged.

Fiona Wilson

FIRST LINE

Where are you, faithless, in all this darkness?
This punch-drunk light won't give you up,
won't tell me where you are, or from,

if it's *you* that loiters in the doorframe,
coming or going, with a cut on your lip
and a blindfold over the darkest of dark eyes.

Kirsti Wishart

L'OUISEAU MECHANIQUE

On entering Monsieur Pichancourt's House of Wonders, the first thing to strike Clement Braun as strange was birdsong. Such bright and natural music was only ever heard in the city's spacious and leafy public parks and to hear it indoors was disorientating. After adjusting to his surroundings Clement realised the trills and elegant whistles were real. Through an open doorway at the end of a corridor leading toward the back of the shop he glimpsed golden cages and fluttering, brightly-coloured wings. He would now be able to verify the rumour that Pichancourt kept an aviary and menagerie in order to study the movement of birds and animals, the better to replicate their movements.

After spending minutes alone examining the mechanical toys on display, Clement began to wonder when he would be joined by his mysterious host. It had taken some time for this meeting to be arranged. A notice in the window advertised opening times along with a telephone number, but they bore no relation to the actual hours the shop was open. Although they discussed its supposed contents at length, none of Clement's regular clientele had entered the shop. Potential customers who had dialled the phone number were greeted by a heavily-accented answerphone message asking them to leave Monsieur Pichancourt their contact details and he would return their call to arrange an appointment. Invariably they waited and heard nothing.

When Braun had visited the shop for a fourth time and found, yet again, its windows dark and its door locked he had despaired of ever meeting the legendary toymaker. Staring at the tantalising objects on display he was sure he could see a light coming from a back room and imagined the craftsman too absorbed in his work to worry about losing a sale. Clement had returned to his office and rang the number, left a message in French and, a short time later, the phone rang with an excitable Frenchman on the end of it, speaking in his native tongue so quickly Braun had difficulty understanding him.

'Clement Braun! Finally! My most sincere apologies at not having contacted you myself but I was not sure how a great man such as yourself would respond to an overture from someone like me, a newcomer to the city.'

For a moment Clement thought Monsieur Pichancourt had perhaps mistaken him for somebody else. It was true that he was one of the most respected toyshop owners of the city. His were the shops parents took their children to find the toys they had loved when they were young and he took pride in his ability to construct with his own hands any toy or game requested. But Clement, a modest man, felt his reputation hardly warranted the praise that Monsieur Pichancourt, one of the greatest automaton artists recent times had seen, heaped upon him.

Clement had scarcely believed the rumours that had begun to circulate in Braun's Robotics that Pichancourt was about to open a shop in the city and, moreover, the great man himself would work within it. Pichancourt was rightly regarded as an extraordinary continental craftsman and his work had always been sold as individual items through agents. The Master had no desire to dirty his skilful hands with commerce. The strange opening times of the shop certainly seemed to bear this out. Furthermore, although Braun's city was famed for its entertainments and love of novelty, what had possessed a notoriously reclusive man to travel hundreds of miles from the small French town of his birth to set up business here?

As he paid closer attention to the machines on display Clement began to notice that for all their obvious beauty many of them were incomplete, as though their maker had grown tired of the ease with which he contrived their movements. Despite this they were the most impressive examples of the mechanical art that he had ever been privileged enough to see. He had gained an original Pichancourt for sale after lengthy and tortuous dealings with one of the Frenchman's most notorious agents, Albrecht. It had been a simple affair of a woodcutter cutting down a tree with a nest of cheeping hatchlings in its branches who, when the tree had fallen, wiped his brow with a handkerchief pulled from a jerkin pocket. Clement, who was usually happy to see his toys leave his shop, and knew the pleasures they would bring, was sorry to see this one go and almost refused the sale.

And then, as he was peering at a machine displaying a lion tamer cracking his whip at three lions, a voice shouted from the corridor, 'Who is there?' Braun turned quickly in shock and as soon as he did so Pichancourt's expression turned from a fierce scowl to a huge welcoming smile and the screwdriver he had been holding in a threatening manner was spun and slipped into one of the many pockets in his long brown work coat. He spread his arms wide and then, a small man, reached up and clapped his hands on Braun's shoulders. His eyes were magpie black, grey bags under them telling of many hours spent working late into the night. His eyebrows were thick and bristling, black hair swept back from his forehead, almost white at the temples. He looked like a man with the skill and determination to build anything his mind and heart set upon and for a moment Clement was disturbed by this sudden knowledge.

'Finally, finally we meet, Clement Braun and Monsieur Pichancourt. History, this day will make toy-making history! Come, come through to the workshop. You must be tiring of these trifles, these excrescencies. I am ashamed that you had to see them but I must give the public something to gawp at.' Clement, who loved all his customers, even the ones who made the most ridiculous demands, was taken aback by this sentiment but was able only to make the meekest noises of protestation as Pichancourt quickly moved him into the corridor he had peered down on arrival. Although he was several feet smaller than Braun, his shoulders were broad and he moved with a darting energy. When he grasped his wrist Clement could feel the strength built up by years of physical work. 'Please, please Mr Braun, take a seat. I have much to tell you. Much.'

He pointed to two seats at the end of a large workbench, cluttered with cogs and bellows, clockmaking and soldering tools in the centre of the small workshop and then left. Clement was only able to glance at the objects set on the shelves lining the walls as he cleared his chosen seat of plans and diagrams before Pichancourt returned carrying a glass of water. He was aware of an astrolabe, a coloured phrenologist's head and beautifully engraved anatomical depictions of birds, lions and humans on the walls pinned beside many photographs and plans of the city. Then the toymaker began to talk with such charisma it was impossible to look away.

'Please, have a sip of water, Mr Braun, I have the feeling

you will need that refreshment later. I do not know if you are fully aware of the circumstances of my leaving the town where I spent much of my life. But the fact of the matter is I was not forced out but chose to leave. Yes, I am aware of the rumours. I have a confession to make to you tonight, Clement Braun. All my life I have been fascinated by the city and yet afraid of it. I have a fear of crowds and so I relied on reports of various cities from agents who visited my workshop. It was due to their stories that I began to formulate my next great project. The most interesting city they spoke of, the one I thought would most truly appreciate the nature of my craft, was this one. They told me of the entertainment arcades, the game-playing, the theatres and the cinemas and they told me of you, Mr Braun. They told me of your wonderful toyshops and how the citizens truly admire and respect the work of the toymaker. And I knew as they spoke of it that I would have to overcome my childish fears one day and visit it.'

Pichancourt paused a moment, gesturing with an outstretched arm to a red-curtained window and the city that lay beyond. He was lost in thought, the expression on his face a peculiar mix of pleasure, excitement and anxiety. Then he remembered his audience and smiled a showman's smile. 'Ah but Mr Braun, I run away with myself. I have something crucial, something vital for you. A gift, a thank you, if I am not being too presumptuous, for the work I think you will be kind enough to assist me with.'

With that Pichancourt left, leaving Braun to wonder if he had translated the last sentence correctly. A few days ago the idea of sitting in Pichancourt's studio listening to the great man hold forth would have been ridiculous enough. For him to be offered the opportunity of working in partnership with him was almost too much to believe and he gazed around the room in an attempt to find something ordinary and mundane to focus on to dissipate the dreamlike atmosphere. But there was nothing banal in Pichancourt's world. There was nothing restful here, but instead objects that caused the mind to race on into flights of association. He began to feel as if he were in an elaborate stage set, as though someone had gained the power of entering the deepest recesses of his imagination and there chose the very items that would cause him wonder.

He was on the point of rising from his chair, throwing back the thick red curtains and opening the window for some cold city air, when Pichancourt returned carrying a large square object, draped in the same red curtain material covering the window. For all its size it appeared light as he placed it carefully to the side of the table where Braun sat. When the Frenchman saw the curiosity in Braun's face he waved a finger from side to side as though warding off a child. 'For later, Mr Braun. You do not have to worry, it will be yours. But first I must talk a little longer, if you will be so kind as to indulge me.

'I have always been interested in the city's interconnected systems, the way that every action has far-reaching consequences, rippling through its citizens. And I began to plan how I would go about building a complete automata city, a machine which I believe would be of great use not only to scientists but to artists also. Who has not had the dream of observing a city from on high, seeing the connections, the paths of energy that lie hidden from us as we travel the streets locked in our individual perspective? Behind this door, Mr Braun,' – Pichancourt pointed behind him to a dark highly-polished door which Clement had not noticed until that moment – 'I have begun my work. It takes up one whole floor of this building, a huge venture that only a madman would attempt,' and he smiled in a way he perhaps believed self-mocking but the gleam in his eye caused Braun's mouth to dry. 'But one which I, as the greatest craftsman of his art, cannot fail to attempt.'

Clement reached for the glass of water Pichancourt had earlier set by his side. He now realised why the workshop was so unusually small. It was a front, the wall and door facing him perhaps not as sturdy as they appeared but sufficient to keep concealed what lay behind. After he had taken a sip, noticed his hand shaking lightly, he asked, in stumbling French, 'This is all very interesting, Monsieur Pichancourt, indeed fascinating, but you must excuse my confusion as to why you would reveal such a grand plan. It is clear from the secrecy surrounding your shop that you are reluctant for the public to discover the means by which you produce your wonderful machines,' Pichancourt nodded, his brow darkening. 'I am most grateful to you for inviting me here but how could I help in your venture? I'm a salesman, that's all.'

'No, Braun, that is not all,' Pichancourt said sharply, taking a deep breath to compose himself before continuing. 'You know this city and you know toys, you treat them with the respect they deserve and the people who buy them, you know and respect *them*. My agents have told me that while there are bigger toymakers and toyshop owners you are the one who knows his clientele the best, whose shops work in close harmony with the moods of the city. And that, that is why I need you. I need you to be my eyes and ears, to notice the movements of the city. I have thrown myself into my City with a passion, working from plans and photographs brought to me by my agents. You will have noticed the half-finished machines, abandoned when I have discovered a new way of rendering the way cherry blossom falls when caught in a May breeze. I still fear the city streets, I am used to small town ways but I am also very aware that I lack something more than the ability to explore the thing that fascinates me. I have the intelligence of a mathematician and the skill of a clockmaker but these are cold, heartless skills whereas you, Clement Braun, have heart. I will provide the machinery of this city but you will provide its soul. You will be my closest contact with the city and in return I will train you in my ways of automata. I have never married, I have no close family and yet I would like my skills to continue. I have read your articles, seen some of your toys and while the movement is a trifle gauche there is great potential. I need a friend here, Braun, an ally, and I believe you are that man.'

At that he lent forward and clasped the wrist of Braun's right hand and looked intently into his eyes, causing the other man to gasp and blush. Slowly, Pichancourt released his grasp, letting his fingers trail. 'Apologies, Mr Braun. I am an impatient man and I have been so eager to meet you that I fear I have rushed into matters you will need some time to digest. I think it might be best if you leave shortly to consider my proposal for us to form an alliance. And here. I would like you to take this gift with you. This is not to blackmail you, believe me. You have been very helpful to me for many years, selling my work in this city, spreading my reputation in your country. I feel you deserve this whether you decide to help me with my current project or not.' With that he unveiled the object he had brought in.

L'OUISEAU MECHANIQUE

A curved gold bird cage like the ones Braun had seen holding the birds as he was led along to this room. But the bird this cage held, in its absolute stillness, was obviously fake. An automaton perched with its head cocked, its right eye made of a stone or glass bead that appeared black but glinted red when caught by the light. It was fantastically decorated, the head a brilliant green, the beak gold, a breast of sapphire flecked with silver, the wings midnight blue, the tail royal purple, feathers metal but so finely wrought they imitated reality perfectly. 'I have a weakness for the garish, Mr Braun, but people seem to like it. I fear the drab and boring,' Pichancourt said before clicking a switch at the base of the cage. At first, the bird remained still before a gentle humming and whirring began. Slowly the bird's head turned to face Braun, its beak opened and it began to sing, body and wings moving to accompany its song.

Braun was not an appreciator of music. While he did attend concerts with friends he was often puzzled by their powerful reactions to a piece of chamber music. While they spoke of its tenderness and delicacy he would show them the new design he had been busy sketching on the back page of the programme. But when he heard this bird's song he felt tears start in his eyes. It was like a distillation of all the finest examples of birdsong, from a lark ascending to a blackbird's call at dusk to a nightingale heard through a hushed evening shared with a loved one. It was supremely artificial: no bird on earth could produce such a sound and it was therefore sublime, unearthly. This impression was enhanced by the bird's movement as its wings, tail and head moved with a fluidity and swiftness Braun had never, in his many years in the toy trade, seen before. He wondered whether or not Pichancourt had played an illusionist's trick, substituting a real bird for the automaton he had first seen. But no bird could be decorated in such a way and no bird could be trained to perform the song issuing from the cage.

When it had reached a crescendo Pichancourt adjusted a lever set next to the switch and the bird ruffled its feathers, shuffled along its perch and then hopped, moving its wings to adjust to its new position on the lower perch, lent back and spread its wings for a moment, showing their rosepink undersides, before they folded back into place. It then dropped to the bottom of the cage and pecked and scratched at the bits of straw and seeds that were scattered there. Braun was aware of Pichancourt easing a switch back, there was the murmured whirring once again and the bird's movement slowed and stopped.

A silence fell on the room, a silence that follows the moment when a great and unexpected secret changing everything has been told. It was broken by Pichancourt. 'A mere token, as you can see, but I would be very happy for you to take it. A gift. It's easy to control, the switches and levers at the back are self-explanatory.' He picked up the red cloth and covered the cage, stood up and held out his hand. 'Now, I am afraid I must return to my work. It has been wonderful to meet you, Clement Braun.'

Braun, who had been held transfixed, felt the hair rise on the back of his neck, shivered and blinked, afraid. What he had seen was impossible. No machine could replicate the movements of a bird in such eerily natural fashion but he had heard the movements of a mechanism. He felt himself stand up, his hand shaken by Pichancourt before being shown back through the shop to the front door. Pichancourt handed him the cage to open the door for Braun and when he turned, Braun grasped the cage to his chest, expecting the Frenchman to realise he had made a mistake and attempt to take the bird from him. Pichancourt noted this and smiled as though something had been confirmed. 'No Mr Braun, it is yours. I will be in touch again shortly with further details,' and then Clement found himself out in the fresh air of the street, listening to bolts and ratchets being set in place behind him.

Later that night he sat in the leather chair of his study with a large glass of brandy in one hand, the other drumming nervously on the small side table to his left on which the cage sat, still covered by the red curtain. An ambition he had held of working with the Master since seeing his first Pichancourt automaton when eight years old had come true. Here was his opportunity to achieve toymaking's greatest accolade. Yet he was deeply unsettled by the events of the past few hours. He thought of Pichancourt's room, concealed from everyone's eyes but Pichancourt's, housing a city in miniature. He got up from his chair and walked over to the window which granted him a view of rooftops and city streets. Perhaps because of the alcohol he had the queer sensation that his movement had been preordained, that some concealed track and pulley had led him to where he now stood. He left his vantage point abruptly and sat back in the chair. It was a scheme driven by madness, impossible, unachievable but that was what made it wonderful and so very attractive. A folly, yes, but a grand one.

Inevitably, he felt his eyes drawn to the covered cage. With one hand he pulled gently at the bottom of the red material then stopped. If the bird was there he would have to believe what Pichancourt was capable of. If the bird was not there his heart would break. He would have another glass of brandy. He would wait until he knew his mind a little better; and then, perhaps, the bird would sing and sing for him alone.

Olga Wojtas

THE BALLAD OF THE STARBUCKS CAFÉ

Hail to me, the Starbucks barista. I'm God in this place, ever present, all seeing, ignored by most.

There are the ones who give me my due, say 'please' and 'thank you', and leave 20p in the glass dish. But even they, once they find a seat and put down their bags of shopping, forget I'm there. And even with them, the nice ones, I may give them the Granola bar with the corner missing, or a chicken panini that's past its date. I see myself more as the Old Testament-style God, unpredictable and really rather vindictive. Just because you obey the rules doesn't guarantee that it's all going to go well for you.

Not that I automatically give the best to those who don't deserve it. The guy who didn't even look at me as he barked: 'Tuna melt and a skinny decaf grande latte,' got full fat milk and caffeine with an extra shot. They very rarely realise. They think because they're given choices that they're somehow in control, and that what they get is what they asked for. With the few who have unusually discerning taste-buds, I'm either harassed and apologetic or slow-witted and apologetic. I've never had any trouble.

When I took the guy's tuna melt over to him, I found he was sitting on the sofa with a rather fraught young woman who'd come in about 20 minutes earlier. That is, she'd been fraught then; now she was nestling into him with a kittenish contentment. He had an arm round her and a mobile phone in his other hand.

'It's a nightmare here,' he was saying. 'Have dinner without me. The amount of work I've still got to get through, God knows when I'll get home.'

God knows everything, I thought. His left hand lay casually on her shoulder and her left hand had crept upwards to caress it. She wasn't wearing a wedding ring, but he was. Between them, they were breaking a fair few of the rules.

They chose us for their rendezvous, she arriving first, eager and nervous, he sauntering in, certain of her. She was as polite to me as her anxiety allowed, but he was dismissively abrupt. He always ordered a skinny decaf grande latte and he always got full fat milk and caffeine with an extra shot. They never stayed particularly long: presumably it was geographically convenient to meet here before going on to her place. I reckon that either her flat wasn't well-equipped or she wasn't much of a cook since he always ate a tuna melt along with the latte. I generally managed to introduce one contaminant or another before taking it over to him. He never said thank you.

It wasn't that he was smitten with her, more that he saw her adoration as his due. She would sit gazing at him, her lips slightly parted in wonder that he was here beside her. She listened carefully when he spoke, spoke herself when he wanted to be amused, kept quiet when he wanted to relax. How very different a mistress is from a wife. He luxuriated in her attentiveness, happy to be her god. A mistake on both their parts.

As the weeks went by, the body language changed. She grew less pliant, he less rigid. It wasn't that they were merging into a single contour, more that she was growing in power. There was apparently something that she wanted, and I watched her shift from wheedling to requesting to demanding. He was visibly diminishing. But it didn't make him any more civil, so I didn't alter his order. After I brought him his panini, I hovered around, clearing and wiping nearby tables, long enough to discover that she was insisting that he move in with her. He didn't care for the idea at all, but he couldn't see a way out.

Then they both disappeared. I had others to occupy me; I didn't think about them overmuch. But I felt a gush of pleasurable recognition when he turned up suddenly, looking tired and weighed down.

'Tuna melt and a skinny decaf grande latte,' he snapped without looking at me, but it was so much bluster. And then – they still surprise me sometimes – he went to join a well-dressed woman sitting stiffly on an upright wooden chair. The wife, not the mistress. After I brought him his panini, I hovered around, clearing and wiping nearby tables, long enough to discover that he was pleading to come back. And she was insisting he stay away. She drank her coffee briskly (regular macchiato, just as she'd asked), then left without a backward glance.

Despite the inflexibility of the wooden chair, he slumped. He took out his mobile phone and made a call. He needed comfort. I made a full fat caffeinated latte, added two extra shots and took it over to him.

'Skinny decaf, on the house,' I said.

He took it and muttered something; it was difficult to tell whether he was thanking me or not.

It was about 20 minutes before she arrived (the mistress, not the wife) but his panini was still unfinished, with congealed mozzarella oozed over the plate. He looked up at her so eagerly, so expectantly, hoping she would be his salvation since he could find none elsewhere.

And then I was distracted by a group of young people, laughing, exuberant, playful, determined to enjoy every minute. They made me smile.

I was still dealing with them when I heard a thud. He had fallen from the chair and was lying on the floor, his face grey and sheened with sweat. The mistress gave a small disbelieving screech, and whirled round towards the counter.

'For God's sake, call an ambulance!' she cried.

And I thought, oh yes, now you turn to me. Now you realise I have the power of life and death.

BIOGRAPHIES

Tom Bryan was born in Canada, 1950, of Irish/Scottish homesteading background. Long-resident in Scotland. Widely-published and broadcast poet, fiction and non-fiction writer. Has appeared previously in *New Writing Scotland* over the years. Lives in Caithness.

Jim Carruth was born in Johnstone in 1963 and has spent most of his adult life living in Renfrewhire. A widely published poet, his first collection *Bovine Pastoral* was published by Ludovic Press in 2004.

Ken Cockburn: former Assistant Director at the Scottish Poetry Library, for whom he recently co-edited *Intimate Expanses: XXV Scottish Poems 1978–2002*. Now working freelance, and as a director of platform projects, the successor company to pocketbooks. The sequence, 'On the fly-leaf of...: a bookshelf', was shortlisted for the Deric Bolton Long Poem Award in 2003.

Neil Cocker was born in Falkirk in 1972 and lives in the Netherlands. He has had stories published in *Original Sins* (Canongate Prize Anthology 2001) and *NWS 21*. He has almost finished his first novel, *The Vodka Angels*, which is about a Scot teaching English badly in a Lithuanian ghost-town.

Michael Coutts' stories range from the sad or humorous to the deeply mad. He is now sweating over his first novel, is married, has four daughters and lives in Edinburgh.

James Cressey: born in Edinburgh, educated at George Heriot's school. After degrees at Edinburgh and London he taught Latin for several years before moving to Sicily. He now lives in Palermo writing short fiction in English and Italian.

Alexander J. Cuthbert, originally from Cellardyke in the East Neuk, has worked in Special Education for the last eleven years and is currently studying at the University of Glasgow. Shortlisted in 2003 and 2004 for the RSAMD

Edwin Morgan Poetry Prize. Co-founder of The Seer Press.

Vicki Feaver moved to Scotland in 2001, settling in Dunsyre at the edge of the Pentlands. She has published two collections of poetry, *Close Relatives* (1981) and *The Handless Maiden* (1994) which won a Heinemann Prize, was short-listed for the Forward Prize and also gained her a Cholmondeley Award. A new collection, *The Book of Blood*, is due from Cape in Spring 2006.

Graham Fulton's published poetry collections include *Humouring the Iron Bar Man*, *Knights of the Lower Floors* (both Polygon) and *Ritual Soup and other liquids* (Mariscat). A new collection called *Flying Lessons* is finished and two others, *Think Positive* and *Saved Messages*, are almost completed.

Galway-based writer **Rab Swannock Fulton**'s work has appeared in *Chapman*, *Northwords*, *Poetry Ireland Review*, *Cyphers*, *Criterion*, *The Herald*, etc. His web-novel TRANSFORMATION was launched at the 2005 Múscailt Arts Festival, and can be read, along with his other work, at: **http://frink.nuigalway.ie/~rab**. The website is sponsored by NUI, Galway Arts Office.

Robin Fulton's most recent publications include a batch of poems (*Poetry Scotland* 26), a revised edition of Robert Garioch's *Collected Poems* (Birlinn), translations of Tomas Tranströmer (Bloodaxe), Henrik Nordbrandt (Dedalus) and Olav H Hauge (Anvil), and groups of poems in Chinese, German, Hebrew, Spanish and Swedish.

Iain Galbraith's poems have appeared in *PN Review*, *Chapman*, *The Times Literary Supplement*, *Stand* and *New Writing Scotland*. A selection will appear in *Birches in the City Square*, ed. Andy Brown, Stride Books, 2005. In 2004 he won the John Dryden Prize for Literary Translation, awarded jointly by the British Centre for Literary Translation and British Comparative Literature Association.

Mark Gallacher was born in 1967 in Girvan. Since 1999 he has lived in Denmark. He has a young son and a baby on the way. Poems, prose, short stories have appeared regularly in many quality UK literary magazines, and in Italy and the USA.

Paul Gorman is 30 and grew up in Fife. He studied English at Dundee University and worked in London before returning to Edinburgh, where he lives with his wife. His work has appeared in *Cutting Teeth* and *Riverrun*, and he was shortlisted for the 2002 Dundee Book Prize.

Rody Gorman was born in Dublin in 1960 and now lives in the Isle of Skye. He has published numerous poetry collections in English, Irish and Scottish Gaelic, with *Zonda? Khamsin? Sharaav? Camanchaca?* forthcoming from Leabhraichean Beaga in 2006. He has worked as writing fellow at Sabhal Mòr Ostaig in Skye and at University College Cork and is editor of the annual Irish and Scottish Gaelic poetry anthology *An Guth*.

Originally from Baillieston, Glasgow, **Charlie Gracie** now lives with his family in Thornhill near Stirling. His poetry and short stories have appeared in a number of publications in the last few years, including *Cutting Teeth*, *Pushing Out The Boat*, *Poetry Scotland*, *New Writing Scotland 19, 20* and *21* as well as featured in George Square during Glasgow's 2004 Block Architectural Festival. His work is about dark places and the glimmer that lives there and about green places and what lies beyond the surface.

Rosemary Hector has had writing published in anthologies and magazines since the 1980s and has lived in Northern Ireland, the West Country and the Midlands, returning to Scotland with her family in 1998. Her background is teaching and she now works as a project co-ordinator for NHS Scotland.

Kate Hendry has had a number of poems and stories published in magazines. She teaches in prisons and lives in Ayrshire.

Born and raised in Germany, **Sonja Henrici** moved to

Brighton in 1994 and has lived in Edinburgh since 1999. Prose and poetry published in *Don't Think of Tigers* (ed. Peter Guttridge, 2001). She also writes screenplays and makes films. Her first novel, *The Birthday*, was completed in 2004. www.sonjahenrici.com

John Heraghty lives and works in Glasgow. His first published piece of writing was 'When Stevie Was Married' which appeared in the compilation *Open Ink: A Fictional Guide to Scotland*. The story was subsequently broadcast on Radio Four earlier this year.

Duncan Jones lives in Glasgow. He writes intermittently and haphazardly, and has submitted various things to various publications without success, until now. If he keeps it up Joseph H. Presswell could become an FRGS, too.

Beth Junor is a poet and non-fiction writer. She lives in Edinburgh.

Kirsten Kearney is a N. Irish-bred, Scottish-based PhD student, writer, lecturer and social activist. Her work deals with national identity, music and orality, translation and balladry. Her first volume of poetry, *The Further Tree* (2001) came second in the 2001 Calum MacDonald Memorial Award for poetry pamphlet publishing.

Lis Lee is a poet and playwright of Anglo-Irish-Spanish descent. She lives and works in the Scottish Borders. In 2004 she was awarded a Scottish Arts Council New Writers Bursary. A first collection of poetry *Sob Sister* was published in 2005 by Selkirk Lapwing Press.

Joanna Lilley enjoys experimenting with prose poems and trying to balance brevity with density. She also tries to write novel-sized prose. A graduate of Strathclyde and Glasgow Universities' creative writing MLitt, Joanna lives in the village of Torphichen, West Lothian, and works as a publications manager in Edinburgh.

Stuart Macdonald was born and brought up in South West Scotland. He currently lives in Edinburgh with his wife and two children where he works as a data librarian at Edinburgh University. He's been published widely in numerous publications and hopes that this year sees the publication of a first collection.

Morag McDowell was brought up in Possilpark, Glasgow and went to Strathclyde University. She writes mostly short stories though at the moment she is working on a novel. She has been published in *New Writing Scotland*, *Cutting Teeth*, *Mslexia*, the Bloomsbury/Asham Award winners anthology 2004 and elsewhere.

James McGonigal is a teacher and poet based in Glasgow, writing there and in Ireland. He is a founding editor of SCROLL (Scottish Cultural Review of Language and Literature) published by Rodopi (Amsterdam and New York). His most recent collection is the trilingual long poem *Passage/An Pasaiste*, from Mariscat Press in 2004.

Mora Maclean was born in Glasgow (1960), and studied at Glasgow University. Her first post-graduation job once involved chasing a 'gorilla' across half-time Firhill while dressed as a Keystone Cop! A counsellor by profession, she is also the carer of an elderly relative. She has had poems published in *Cutting Teeth*, etc.

Tony McLean: lazy, good for nothing, he'll come to nothing. Stories previously published in *New Writing Scotland* 19, *Glasgow Kiss* and *Cutting Teeth*. Cut down to about one story per year in the hope that he'll eventually kick the filthy habit. Currently working in the care industry.

Neil McRae: I am originally from the Borders, but now live in Skye. I have been a practising vet for twenty years. I came to Gaelic through love of hill-walking in the Highlands. The great Gàidhlig language will soon be dead, despite (or perhaps because of) the taxpayers' millions. What are we going to do about it?

Lyn Moir's *Me and Galileo* (2001) and *Breakers' Yard* (2003) are published by Arrowhead Press. She writes a lot about seabirds because she lives on the harbour in St.

Andrews. She was awarded a Hawthornden Fellowship in 2004.

Michael Munro was born in Glasgow, works as a freelance lexicographer and editor. Stories and poems in various anthologies and magazines. Wrote *The Patter* and its sequels, and *Clichés and How to Avoid Them* (Chambers).

Presently teaching in Sgoil Lionacleit, Benbecula, **Donald S. Murray** has appeared in *New Writing Scotland* on a number of previous occasions. His short story collection *Special Deliverance* was shortlisted for a Saltire Award a number of years ago. His pamphlet *West Coasters* was also recently shortlisted – this time for the Calum MacDonald Memorial Award.

Siùsaidh NicRath was born and brought up in Embo, Sutherland. She lives in Lochalsh and presently works in the Library at Sabhal Mòr Ostaig, the Gaelic College. She originally trained as a dentist but gave up to look after her four children. A great insomniac, she makes up stories whilst lying awake at night.

Chris Powici lives in Dunblane. He teaches at Stirling University and The Open University. His poetry, which is usually about animals, has appeared in various magazines. He was awarded an SAC New Writers Bursary in 2002, and first prize in the 2003 BBC Wildlife Poet of the Year Awards.

Sarah Reynolds is a Glasgow native, owned by one rather portly cat who resides mainly on the window ledge. She is a member of Maryhill Writers and has contributed poetry and short stories to anthologies.

R.J. Ritchie has organised Stirling Writers Group since 1993. He has had poems published in a range of Scottish and English magazines. Aspiring to write a novel. More into jeux d'esprit than the sloughs of gritty realism, recent poems have been inspired by a growing collection of soft-textile puffins.

Lydia Robb writes poetry in English and Scots. Published in various anthologies including two Polygon *Shorts* collections. Recipient of several literary prizes. Awarded Scottish Arts Council Writer's Bursary in 1998. Poetry collection *Last Tango with Magritte* launched in 2001. Shortlisted for the Scotsman/Orange short story prize 2004.

Kirsteen Scott was born and brought up in Mid-Argyll and graduated MA from Glasgow University years ago. Now wife, mother and grandmother, she describes herself as a lazy writer who snatches at odd ideas and writes for the surprise of what comes. Has had two short stories and two poems published in *Cencrastus*.

Robert Swift lives in Peebles with his wife and four children. He keeps them entertained with pastimes which include moving the garden pond around, and short-lived urges to try something different, bagpipe playing being the most recent. He has had several works published by Polygon, Fish and small presses.

Judith Taylor comes from Perthshire, but now lives and works in Aberdeen. Her poetry has been published in various magazines including *Poetry Scotland*, *Raindog* and *Mslexia*.

Sheila Templeton was born in Aberdeenshire and brought up in the North East. She now lives right beside the sea in Ayrshire, which 'still feels like dancing at a surprise party.' The beach dancing led to a first poetry collection *Slow Road Home*, Makar Press, 2004. Her poems have also appeared in *The Herald*, *Poetry Scotland*, *Poetry Monthly*, *New Writing Scotland* and on Radio Scotland.

Tim Turnbull lives in Perthshire. He was born in North Yorkshire in 1960. He worked in forestry for many years and completed the MA in Creative Writing at Sheffield Hallam University in 2002. In the summer of 2004 he participated in the Poesie der Nachbarn Project in Germany and was awarded an SAC Bursary to help with the completion of a second collection, *Caligula on Ice*. He was appointed Writer in Residence at HMYOI Werrington in October 2004. After two pamphlets, *Work* (Mews Press 2001) and *What was that?* (Donut Press 2004) his first full collection *Stranded in Sub-Atomica* is due from Donut Press in October 2005.

Fiona Ritchie Walker was born and brought up in Montrose and now lives in NE England. She has published two poetry collections: *Lip Reading* (Diamond Twig, 1999) and *Garibaldi's Legs* (Iron Press, 2005). Her short stories have appeared in magazines and anthologies including *Bracket* (Comma Press). She was awarded a Northern Promise Award in 2004.

Fiona Wilson's poems and essays have appeared most recently in *Poetry Review*, *Northwords*, *Pequod*, and *Painted, Spoken*. Her work was featured in *New Writing Scotland 10*. She lives in New York City and teaches at Bard College.

Kirsti Wishart has a PhD in Scottish Literature from the University of St Andrews. She now lives and works in Edinburgh.

Olga Wojtas was born in Edinburgh to a Scottish mother and a Polish father. After graduating in English from Aberdeen University, she joined the *Aberdeen Evening Express* as a reporter. She is now back in Edinburgh, where she is Scottish editor of the *Times Higher Education Supplement*.